CRYSTAL CLEAR

ADVERSITY AS A GIFT

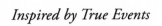
Inspired by True Events

CRYSTAL CLEAR

ADVERSITY AS A GIFT

by KIRK D. DODGE

Copyright © 2018 Kirk D. Dodge

Printed in the United States of America
by Cushing-Malloy, Ann Arbor, Michigan

10 9 8 7 6 5 4 3 2 1

Cover artwork by Gene Rantz of Northport, Michigan.
His work can be seen at www.GeneRantz.com.

Library of Congress CIP Data is on File

ISBN: 978-0-692-08322-2

All inquires should be addressed to:
   PO Box 832
   2300 N. Scenic Hwy
   Lake Wales, FL 33859

To Laurie Riegle, a woman of enterprise, sunshine, and a love for living, beyond which I ever thought possible.

– CONTENTS –

— ACKNOWLEDGMENTS —

Thank you to Don Placek and Keith Witmer for bringing meaning and depth to this effort through their patience and brilliant illustrations. Their art served as fuel.

My children inspire me every day with the purity of their efforts and inspiration. Thank you Mark, Lindsey, and Sam.

— ABOUT THIS BOOK —

Crystal Clear is a collection of childhood and adult remembrances, reminiscences, and reflections about golf and life. Primarily, however, this is a book about family—mine—and how it shaped me and my beliefs as I grew into middle age.

The book is divided into three parts. Part I, Back Nine: Open Mind of a Child, is about the back nine holes of Crystal Downs golf course near Lake Michigan, where I played golf with my dad during my childhood, and what he and those holes taught me. This part of the course is pure Michigan, with its forests and sandy meadows. I start *Crystal Clear* with the back nine because that is how my dad always played the course. If we could sneak in a few holes before dinner, we began on the tenth hole.

Part II, Front Nine: Adult Mind of a Teacher, includes my memories of playing the first nine holes of "the Downs"—a typical Scottish seaside layout—viewed through the lens of the teacher I have become.

Part III, Adversity as a Gift: These stories form a collection of personal triumphs over obstacles, hardships and traumas. These are their stories.

I hope you find clarity within these pages.

— INTRODUCTION —

Looking out from the eastern shore, a little north of the harbor towns of Frankfort and Elberta, Lake Michigan seems to stretch into infinity. High ground offers its own long perspective. Viewers might think there is nothing on the other side—a limitless expanse, a blank canvas upon which they can paint whatever they might wish.

The possibilities appear endless: culture, personal expression, the achievement of dreams. The potential for success and tragedy, exploration, adventures and discoveries—even love—are available to anyone.

When I gaze upon this truly American lake, the only Great Lake to lie completely within the United States, I am magically taken back to my childhood and to the adventures I shared with my mother, my father, and my grandfather: puppies and golf clubs, baseballs and painted walls, parochial schools and public education, and many more experiences both pleasant and otherwise. Such was life as the eldest son of Donny and Margarethe, and the big brother of Glenn. As you explore this memoir, you will come to know an everyday guy and the man who started all of this terrestrial love—my father's father, Donnell Avery, and his typical American family.

Terroir describes how nature influences fine wine and its taste, as groundwater passes through the soil and plant life, it brings fruit trees and hardwoods onto the palette. Winemakers understand that what lives around a vineyard influences the taste of its vintages. A family and its culture can be altered subtly in much the same, enduring way. A grandfather, a father's father, can stand like a broad burr oak, providing shade to rows of vine-ripened grapes.

This book is rooted in terroir—a spiritual landscape of soil, sand, soul, sunshine and darkness that divined for this young boy a world intertwined by love, language, and culture. A fusion—and sometimes a *confusion*—of mind, body, and spirit as old as time itself. This is also a story about looking at what we don't want to see—and understanding it.

— PART I —
BACK NINE: Open Mind of a Child

1

Silent Invitation

Dad put his hands together in a "Vardon V" and made a sweeping motion from quarter past the hour to quarter to, silently asking me, "What do you say we head to Crystal and hit some golf balls?" He didn't need to say the words out loud; my wide green eyes heard him very clearly. We had our own language, one that covered a mass of ground in those few, short, graceful movements.

Grandpa's sawed-down McGregor golf clubs seemed like a novelty then, but spending time with Dad never did. I just nodded. Time with Dad—Donny, as his friends knew him—came as easy as breathing in and breathing out. It just happened.

Golf club storage meant the trunk of dad's smoke blue '63 Thunderbird convertible. As soon as I laced up my PF Flyers, we slipped out the back door of the cottage. Dad engaged the motor for the convertible roof, which always folded itself a bit too loudly into the rear storage boot. That noisy mechanism reliably brought mom to the sandy driveway next to the family cottage.

"What about *dinner*?" she asked, rolling her eyes. Thank God for aluminum foil!

Mom's experimental cooking could stay warm in the oven. We were gone.

In late June, twilight golf in northern Michigan can feel like playing under the midnight sun, where the sun shines late into the evening in this northern clime. "Midnight sun" is also a damn-near-perfect description of the love of my poorly matched parents.

You could see it, you knew it was there, but it didn't generate much warmth.

In those days, golf didn't include carts with beer and GPS. "Par" was a standard of conduct, not a number on a card. Leaving behind handicap and the mendacity of obsessing about scores, walking into golf as architecture creates a pace and domain of its own. Sandpipers still swoop down through the dunes and the ground moves under your feet. They call the course Crystal Downs for a reason—one that would take me years to understand.

Mom loved Crystal and the towns of Frankfort and Elberta as a whole. My dad loved the golf course. He figured out that most people knew little of Dr. Alister Mackenzie's eighteen holes nestled between Crystal Lake and Lake Michigan. Law school in Ann Arbor, and golf on the university's course—also designed by Mackenzie, had introduced Dad to the good doctor's immense talents. But it was the Downs that captured his heart.

This was 1967, and the golfing world was still unfamiliar with what Mackenzie and the good doctor's junior intern, Perry Maxwell, had created on this short stretch of sandy dune grass he dubbed "downs land." Dad knew a judge in Detroit who belonged to the club at Crystal Downs, so admittance was merely showing up to pay your $5.00 to the pro shop man and go play.. (or membership just meant coming up with $250).

We threw our bags over our right shoulders and waved as we passed the golf cottage. We walked in a world where lingering raindrops from a late-afternoon shower glistened through the piney sand. We stood on the tenth tee, plotting our first drives. Dad always started on the tenth. He recognized that the front nine earned Crystal Downs its reputation as a classic Scottish-style course. The back nine just seemed like pure Michigan, which also explained Donny pretty thoroughly: pure Michigan. At the time, I barely understood the difference between the two groups of holes. But, if Dad loved the back nine, then so did I. We were together and that's all that mattered. To the south and east, Crystal Lake shimmered in the long-shadowed sunlight. The world seemed crystal clear perfect.

The tenth tee places you *very* high above the fairway. It's an easy, forgiving tee shot because of its height. You're just getting started, so however well you strike the ball, Sir Isaac Newton gives you a big helping hand. A so-so drive can turn out pretty damn well because gravity and the hard, sandy turf keep the ball rolling.

So art mimics life. Natural architecture permeates the open mind, the child mind.

In the beginning, you don't know any better. Like the first tee on the tenth, everything seems easy. The first test comes with that second shot, trying to stay below the hole and remain on the treacherously left to right tilted green. As in life, it's impossible to avoid trouble altogether. If you're alive, stuff happens. It's not really any body's fault, but eventually, you'll step in it.

Childhood shouldn't be too easy. It should toughen you up for what's ahead.

That's when parents do what parents do. They pick up the pieces when life deals you bad cards. One of my first bad cards was an obstetrician who thought high forceps should be used regularly and liberally during childbirth. My poor mother gasped at how bruised and misshapen I looked when they brought her newborn son to her to be nursed. Occasionally, the doctor forgot the anesthesia—like when he performed the series of cuts that marked me as a nice Semitic baby boy.

When people tell me I'm a tough man to know, they really have no clue.

Life during those early years offered up both soothing and jarring memories. As young as I was, during those blue-hour twilight rambles on the Downs, I felt a growing awareness that my dad carried some heavy baggage. Warmed by our time together, I could sense the charged, edgy past that Donny kept just under his emotional turf. With his sandy brown hair and pale blue eyes, his optimism seemed a bit corny and brittle at times.

Although camouflaged by hope and good intentions, Donny could fool me only for so long. Eventually, all would be exposed to the bright sunlight. First, we went to the dark places.

What happens next evolves into the harsh reality of difference. As you stride from the tenth green to the eleventh tee, nature seems to close in around you. It's like stepping into an eight-year-old's vision of a primordial forest, except this one includes some of the most spiritual, hallowed ground a young mind can conceive. Its seven holes on the way to heaven. Maybe, it's heaven itself. Then, the last hole drops you back into the real world.

That's the beginning. The tenth hole takes you bounding into life, and that's when it starts to get tough. The next eight holes may just leave you speechless. But, I doubt it. Everyone has a story.

2

Consilience

Essentially, the human mind operates as a video camera, constantly taking images and filing them away in sub-cranial storage. Sweet memories stay on top; traumas, both macro and micro, get buried in our emotional bunkers. In the words of writer Thomas Merton, "Every moment and every event of every man's life plants something on every man's soul." Get near that bunker, and you can feel the charge. Go inside and all hell can break loose. Somewhere along the way, I found that I could stand inside my emotional bunkers, chuckle at my predicament, find a sense of quiet, and play on.

The ability to find a sense of quiet and play on would have been useful to Joe Simpson during the 1991 US Senior Amateur at the Downs. The eleventh hole may only play 184 yards on the ground; however, the green slants—steeply from back to front in three tiers. When they cut the cup near the upper middle "fold," which runs from left to right, bisecting the green, scores can climb—as can tempers. Such was the plight of poor Mr. Simpson in the '91 Senior Amateur. During the medal-play portion, he carded a seven as he played a one-man game of ping pong on the green. He asked the caddie to put his bag down and then he started walking with his bag—not to the twelfth tee, but to the parking lot.

Years later, at a USGA cocktail party (walking off the course had disqualified him from USGA competition for two years), Mr. Simpson spotted a Crystal Downs club tie behind a tall gin and tonic.

"You a member at Crystal Downs?" Joe inquired.

"Yes, for quite some time," responded the former club president.

"You guys ever fix that godforsaken eleventh green? Tell me that you fixed the damn thing."

"Excuse me…" retorted the old President.

"Come on, tell me you fixed the damn thing" from Joe again.

"Well, Joe, we did make one change. We widened the walking path from the putting green to the parking lot."

Dad laughed at this story because he understood the emotional swale in which Mr. Simpson found himself that day. When I made a bad shot, Dad usually encouraged me: "Think about how good par will feel from there." This phrase was Donny's variation on Ben Hogan's mantra: "It's always about the next shot." Hogan was something of an expert on perseverance in the face of adversity. As a young boy, he'd watched his father, Chester, take his own life.

With such an image recorded in his childhood RAM, the adult Hogan earned a reputation for leather-hide emotional toughness. Growing up dirt poor in Texas and surviving a horrific, near-fatal car crash, Hogan operated with an almost indescribable steely exterior. He lived by navigating around his own emotional bunkers, keeping his father's self-inflicted gunshot wound a secret even from his beloved wife, Valarie. As a homage to his interior, emotional life, Hogan concocted his "Henny Bogman" persona. He knew his demons—knew them well enough to name them. A lot of us do it. Our demons are reflected in that little "child" who comes out as a reactive personality when the situation requires.

Is there a healthier, more transparent approach to confronting emotional pain and trauma? A thoughtful and considered method? Should we hold these disappointments and our emotional damage up for a good look at a healthy distance?

These buried charges—often the fallout from being on the receiving end of someone else's patterns of subrational behavior or absorbing others' repeated psychodrama— can take many forms. A young girl might experience unwanted attention from older boys or older men—advances and overtures only adults should receive. A young boy might be asked to do things with a grown woman that would make your skin crawl. The lies we tell ourselves to lessen the shame, telling dirty jokes or our own bad behavior to deflect the pain, can also fill these bunkers.

In time, I discovered that my dad lived with his own tortured motion picture. One rainy, foggy night, a heavily inebriated man staggered out of a westside Detroit tavern onto Fort Street and into the path of a car driven by my seventeen-year-old father. Although the inquest cleared Donny of wrongdoing for the man's death, that doesn't erase what happened. What flashed through his mind as the man lurched in front of the car? What image recorded itself at that instant?

The word Fort was no longer benign. His attractive girlfriend at the time, and her charged image as he drove the car that killed a man now became permanent storage. Traumatic confusion can tie up these images in knots. Subrational triggers gradually buried themselves in bunkers throughout Dad's emotional landscape as his terroir seeded new growth—some healthy, some not so much.

Maybe all we can do is hold the psychological file up to the light of day—at a healthy distance. We have to look at the baggage before we can understand it. Then, we can think how good par will feel from there. Play on. Such was the consilience of the eleventh hole.

3

Consilium

D onny pulled his tattered hole-by-hole guidebook from his black-leather Mackenzie Walker golf bag. Number twelve carried a simple, concise admonition: "Keep your drive right of the buttonwood tree." Now the buttonwood tree is the sole object to meet the eye on the left side of the fairway. On the surface, this advice is less than helpful. There's deep fescue all down the right side of the fairway and

the rest of the back nine is to the left. Yet "they" (who in the hell *writes* these little books anyway?) tell you to keep your ball *right* of the buttonwood tree. It's like telling a political candidate to keep it right of Margaret Thatcher. Yeah, really? How in the hell are you supposed to do that? Something is not quite what it seems.

What's not quite right could be called *perspective*. Or, to be more precise, *depth perception*. In reality, the landscape plays a trick on your eyes. This should hardly come as a surprise: the good Dr. Mackenzie served as a camouflage officer in the Great War—the world war immediately before Europeans started numbering them. It's kind of cool, actually, to imagine guys carefully arranging fallen trees and bushes, woodpiles, abandoned military equipment, and confiscated civilian property all to deceive the eyes of the enemy. A few tweaks here, a few tweaks there, and your camouflage team turns the negative space of a battlefield into a visual trap.

What a perfect training ground for a future golf architect who would then go on to menace the minds of the greatest golfers in the world at Augusta National—home of the Masters. Similarity, golfers still befuddle themselves in the name of timeless, classic golf architecture at Crystal Downs. A happy meadow of fescue and one very large and very wide buttonwood, and presto—a steady string of golfers standing dutifully on the twelfth tee carve their subrational slices into the deep fescue.

All of this created one very specific problem for Donny. Dad's miss was the high draw that occasionally became the dreaded hook—the often parabolic, masterful miss that went way left. Dad had taken his game one step further. He had mastered the hook as a miss with acceleration. His miss would hook left at a calculus that even Sir Isaac Newton would have admired. Bernie Sanders could not get as far left as old Donny. Let's just say that on twelve, his hook turned a dogleg right from a 165-yard second shot into a 365-yard second shot.

Golf blacksmiths have yet to forge a club sufficient for a 365-yard second shot; a World War I field artillery cannon might not have offered the range Donny often needed. Let's just say that twelve did not fit Donny's ball flight well.

As you begin to walk the twelfth, the depth of the hole starts to become visible. The fairway ("Fair way!" Boy, the creators of golf were kind to themselves!)—turns to the right and voila! Now that buttonwood is on the other side. Any ball to the left now has to be hit over or under—or through—this godforsaken tree. Hence, the admonition from the guidebook—"Keep your drive right of the buttonwood tree."

It's an interesting coincidence that such clear, straightforward advice immediately follows the eleventh hole and its subtle yet tricky (compared to the other treachery Mackenzie and Maxwell built), putting green. It seems unlikely that those leaving eleven in a foul temper take readily to the fine counsel offered in the guidebook. Imagine Joe Simpson carding a seven on a par three, looking at his guidebook, and reading such a clear directive. No wonder he walked off the course. Who volunteers for such abuse?

Well, Donny and his son Kirk not only showed up, we were happy!

One day, when I was much older, it occurred to me: What if a bolt of lightning struck the buttonwood tree and burned it to the ground? What if the advice we were receiving was based on something that no longer existed?

What if things change?

At that moment, I began to think that maybe this perfect guy I call Dad might, someday, change. I wasn't sure what I'd do. I hoped that buttonwood tree would never die. Hence, the consilium of the twelfth hole.

4

Purgatorium

Things that seem interminable rarely last forever. Those too painful to remember rarely go on indefinitely. It is just so as I stand at the thirteenth hole. Thirteen supposedly means that bad luck is preordained. Believe that only if you also believe that good luck comes along with the bad—yin and yang, as with the fates.

Sweet memories of a father stand next to fuller, painful memories. The thirteenth remains a very long, two-shot hole. A primordial forest on the right draws close to the fairway and absorbs the light into its dark shadows. Bunkers, glimpsed through tall fescue, knolls, and hillocks, mine the left. The closer you hit your drive to the forest, (with old stories Sutter Road use to be there), and thus a harder and flatter fairway gives you a shorter and better angle to the green. The fairway rolls out in front of you all the way to the ramp edge of a green you can only sense. It's akin to looking at the edge of a china plate from the side. Except that this china plate fractures in three different directions.

Mind ~ Body ~ Spirit
Father ~ Son ~ Holy Ghost
Earth ~ Wind ~ Fire
Donnell ~ Donny ~ Kirk Donnell

Not long after my grandfather, Tank Corporal Donnell Avery, stood in front of our family-room TV, with tears flowing down his cheeks saluting fellow countrymen Neil Armstrong and Buzz Aldrin as they walked and talked on the moon...he died.

The day your grandpa dies is bad enough. On that day, however, part of my dad died, too.

The third of five sons, Grandpa Don had lost his mother when he was twelve; she died giving birth to his youngest brother, Harold. My grandfather was the son of Ohio's unluckiest dirt farmer, and his lot only became worse when he was offered to another local farmer as cheap labor. Somehow, this local farmer thought it was okay to use young Don as a punching bag for his drunken entertainment—a grim existence, to be sure, until Donnell's brother Paul heard about it and kindly came over to rearrange the farmer's jaw and dental work.

Young Don figured life couldn't get much worse than it was in Bluffton, Ohio. He ran away—and not to Malibu or Miami Beach. No, young Don gathered up his meager belongings and settled in Detroit. It was 1912 and good luck was just around the corner. Enterprising guys started putting boat engines into quadricycles.

The Roaring Twenties brought Don prosperity; a steady, shapely wife; and two strapping sons. Brokering land in and around Detroit between 1920 and 1950 can fairly be described as a perfect profession for a guy with a sixth-grade education, a strong willed wife, and an eternally sunny optimism.

After he'd taught his sons to hunt, fish, and hit a two iron, Donnell Avery convinced himself and anyone who would listen that he was the luckiest man on Earth.

Watching his boys graduate from the university in Ann Arbor seemed almost surreal. How could a motherless kid from Ohio have escaped and created such happiness? How could anyone not love life? This was my grandfather, the father my own father loved.

When two men love one another, the bond can be difficult to put into words. So much never gets said; it doesn't need to. We're men. That's how the guy upstairs wired us—or so we're told. Knowing these two men meant learning that love is not a feeling: it's a behavior. It's learning how to cast a fly, throw a spiral, score a Tiger baseball game, win at marbles, paint a football helmet maize and blue, flight a golf ball, and tend a pin. Stand in the shadow. Know when to be small. Know when not to. Know when to fight. Know when to make peace. Ancestral lessons from Grandpa Don to Donny were taught to me by example.

That rainy night on Fort Street that I described earlier, Donny was driving Grandpa Don's car, a 1949 Packard Station Sedan with windshield wipers prone to wiping out of sequence. One wiper could go a bit lazy. It was the one on Dad's side. Grandpa had meant to have it serviced.

He forgot.

That night, the wiper didn't limp out of a tavern onto a six-lane highway, but it did limp across the windshield. The inquest didn't dwell on the condition of the car. The officers probably didn't even notice. But the two Dons knew. It was part of their bond—two men having each other's back. The problem was, one man was still a boy, and another man was dead. Even a grown man might have been burdened by the weight of this memory.

Lillian Knox had been Donny's girl ever since he first drove her home in his 1940 Ford. Lily should have been carved on the prow of a ship. Sweet and full of moxie, Lily put a hold on Donny's heart that kept him up at night. His camera mind found its way to her warm, ample chest at the very moment the car struck the drunken man—a moment he would never forget, a moment of attraction and revulsion all rolled together under a car in a traumatic confusion that would not let go of him.

On the drive home from Crystal one day, Dad told me that story. I didn't know what to say. I knew Dad wasn't perfect. I'd seen his law school grades. I guess he wanted to help me not to put him up on a pedestal. It didn't work. I loved him even more. He and I both parred thirteen that day. He revealed himself to his son, and the ball disappeared pure into the cup.

Such was the Purgatorium of the thirteenth.

5

Less Is More

Fourteen points you toward God. After the purgatory of thirteen, with its light-swallowing forest, purifying man–boy bunkers, and cracked china plate green, heaven appears on the horizon. Off to the north, the green disappears into rolling, grassy sand dunes. Beyond those dunes, the beach and bay frame the southern opening of the Sleeping Bear National Lakeshore.

It's beautiful in a way that sneaks up on you—no rocky cliffs or crashing waves. This honey sweetens your mind like a perfect woman. Up close, fourteen is a short par three hole, a nine or a wedge to a benign, receptive green. Receptive should under no circumstances be confused with easy. Fourteen loves you—loves you to death.

Maria Giordano appeared in my life long after I fell in love with her—or with the idea of her. Lithe and long, yet only five feet four inches tall, she struck me like every human contradiction that true beauty affords—yin and yang all the way. How could the guy upstairs color eyes blue and brown at the same time? Northern Italy and a cheeky Black Irish mom seemed to be part of the answer.

When your first feelings of attraction end in shame and embarrassment, you really need a warm and sweet resolution of those feelings the next time. A kiss that ends on its own. A hand being held at just the right time. An embrace that slowly awakens you to an intimate whisper. At some point, you need it the way the guy upstairs intended. You need it crystal clear and light.

Is intimacy between two seventeen-year-olds ever healthy? Probably not, and yet it happens every day on our little planet. Less is more takes on special meaning with two young, inexperienced lovers. Can they look each other in the eye comfortably? Can they walk in the park holding hands? Can their intimate whispers evolve slowly into a passionate kiss? If these simple, genuine expressions of romance seem un-comfortable, anything really intense would be a step too far. Somehow, Maria and I could take our own sweet time. Slowly and surely, we seemed comfortable with each step along the way—the path to love.

Back on thirteen, a bunker short of the green swallows up second shots struck a little too quick and a little too fast. About sixty yards from the green, the good Dr. Mackenzie decided this would be where Crystal Downs members would learn to master the most difficult shot in golf.

Sixty-yard pitches require real finesse and tempo. Striking the same intimidating shot from a sandy bunker means you're a god. It's really the Goldilocks of golf shots—not too hard, but not too soft. In Eastern philosophy, it's called the Middle Way. In the Christian world, sixty-yard pitches from sand can rightly be considered golf purgatory—the place where you purify your swing.

Dad dispensed with all that ecclesiastical detail. He kept it simple: "Quiet legs, Kirk. Quiet legs."

It's wise to master this spiritual shot because you need it again on the fourteenth tee. When golf architects cut the hole short, the green small, and the opening smaller, you need very, very quiet legs. You need heavenly tempo. You need a swing that won't hurt anyone, a swing that's easy to watch—that the gods themselves would call pure. Losing yourself to another should be this way. That's how I like to think about it.

Less is more when it comes to the fourteenth.

6

Out and In

Number fifteen at the Downs begins the return for the back nine. In their earliest designs, golf courses would take you "out" and back "in." These originals typically evolved on the fallow land that linked farms to the beach and the sea. Hence, the word *links* entered golf vernacular. *Out* meant walking and hitting until the halfway point.

Turning around and playing back in became the norm. Think of early Scots–Irish tracks like the Old Course at St. Andrews, Royal Troon, Portrush, Dornoch, or North Berwick. *Out* and *in* often made its appearance right onto the scorecard.

In America, golf designs typically come in two nine-hole loops—the first of thirteen principles on golf architecture and written by Mackenzie. At Crystal, the walk from the fourteenth green to the fifteenth tee points you back toward the beginning. As in life, you get to see where you've been, but from a different perspective. Making the turn back over a golf course is both geographic and metaphoric. So it is at the fifteenth tee.

On the card, the fifteenth hole does not look like much. It's not very long. It's fairly straightforward, with very little going on to the casual observer. The head golf professional at Crystal Downs will tell you that during the same 1991 U.S. Senior Amateur when Joe Simpson made himself a Homeric figure in the minds of the Crystal Downs membership, no one birdied the fifteenth hole. How can that be? How can a relatively uncomplicated short hole with just three bunkers be so effective in defending par?

The answer lies with a green and putting surface that rarely allow incoming second shots to end up near the cup. Think of the fifteenth green as an almost imperceptible dome, a subtle little design feature that causes a very definite pattern of unexpected outcomes.

As a parent, and now a grandparent, I've begun to recognize old (and new) patterns. I see the younger and the older Donny in very different lights. My dad was doing the best he could, and doing it well at times. He never gave up. He never quit. The one subtle flaw? He wasn't much for looking candidly and clinically at himself. His pattern of mistakes tended to repeat themselves: taking too much financial risk, borrowing too much to finance investments, and the list goes on. He made those same mistakes over and over again.

The tendency to repeat the same mistakes probably characterizes most of us, unless we have a great awareness of ourselves. Most people, however, are unable to "get out of their own way."

In recent years, research in behavioral psychology has advanced this notion. Essentially, professionals categorize our behavior into three descriptors: rational, suprarational, and subrational.

Rational: Rational behaviors include the everyday duties of brushing our teeth, paying our taxes, and being on time. It's the stuff most of us learn to do by rote.

Suprarational: Suprarational behavior is evidenced by creativity in art, science, language, or sport. The suprarational separates us from most primates. Most of us can find some activity as a creative outlet. I'm writing this story. Alan Turing analogized a "thinking machine" from a seashell. Steve Jobs added calligraphy to personal computers. We analogize from one context to the next and do something original.

Subrational: Subrational behavior includes activities that we undertake but don't experience consciously while we're doing them. Subrational behavior usually leads to repetitive, self-defeating patterns, such as drinking too much, gossiping about others, borrowing too much money, taking careless risks, or simply losing our tempers—like we do on a golf course. Golf really is a metaphor for life.

This last area of subrational behavior bears a bit of closer attention. Old Donny shared a weakness with young Donny. They both liked fast cars and fast women, but what they really shared was a pattern of self-defeating behavior. Its roots might not be hard to unearth. The traumatic conflation of a staggering, inebriated man seen through a rain soaked windshield and the sleek chassis of his high school sweetheart had to affect him deeply—bat shit crazy—whether he knew it or not.

Professionally, Donny built, bought, and sold apartment complexes and a couple of shopping centers. Early on, while still practicing law, he would learn of prize parcels before they became known to the public. Later, he became skilled at finding motivated sellers tired of the headaches of property management. Seeing that pattern in others might have helped him avoid similar mistakes, but Dad seemed unable to resist risk. Ultimately, after taking too much risk too many times, he filed for bankruptcy.

Like all of us, Donny could have used an "out" and "in" mind-set on his own life scorecard.

7

Symmetry of Threes

Number sixteen at Crystal plays clear and clean as a three-shotter. At close to six hundred yards, it's just too long and narrow at the green to go for it with only two shots. Some try, and one or two Herculean types actually say they've succeeded, but just because it can be done, doesn't mean it should be done. Sometimes, it's just better to do it in threes:

Father ~ Son ~ Holy Ghost
Animal ~ Vegetable ~ Mineral
Larry ~ Moe ~ Curly

My dad's prodigious right-to-left draw came in very handy on the sixteenth. The hole stretches along the same hillocks and knolls of tall fescue that border the twelfth and thirteenth holes—terrain we now play in reverse. It sets up to the right and then arcs to the left before dropping down to a green that cuts from front left to back right. Donny would set up his primal right-to-left tomahawk and watch that wee white ball bound its way to three wood range. Presto! Down from three shots to two—basically, the whole key to the game. So, why not do it every time? If it's that straightforward, why not dial one up every time? Because, well, it's hard. It's chancy. Overcook the swing and that tiny ball buries itself in the love grass, the tall fescue on the left, where you really get into trouble.

Doing things in threes involves less risk. It's less chancy. It's logical. It's easy on the mind and on the ear. Peter, Paul, and Mary; red, white, and blue; mind, body, and spirit—not only do they capture the key elements, they sound nice.

Have you ever sat through a truly great speech delivered at a conference or commencement and you become so mesmerized by the speaker you lose track of time? What accounts for that special kind of experience? Is it the message? How it's delivered? The sense of purpose girding the content? Yes, yes, and yes! Powerful messages need to be composed. Great messages are succinct; they're tight and clear. Yet, that's not enough. On June 12, 2005, the late Steve Jobs delivered the Commencement Address at Stanford University. He stated simply, "I want to tell you three stories. Nothing more; just tell three stories: the story of my adoption, the story of my being fired by Apple, the story of my cancer diagnosis."

The symmetry of Jobs's three concise descriptions was compelling, but he read them from a printed page. He knew these stories cold, but *he actually felt the need to read them.* The result was a monotone delivery with no authentic eye contact. His hands held the printed page, which meant that he couldn't use gestures to convey emphasis or intent. The symmetry of the three stories held together what *could have been* an even greater and more effective address. His body language was nonexistent. He simply did not connect with the audience.

Imagine Dr. Martin Luther King's "I Have a Dream" speech delivered without eye contact, variation in voice and tone, or purposeful hand movements. Imagine it without the backdrop of civil rights and the moral imperative to end racial discrimination. Imagine that speech without its profound sense of purpose, its compelling spirit. This legendary speech

became timeless and essential to understanding America in the 1960s because it connected on all three levels: mind, body, and spirit.

Coming of age in the investment industry, I learned a lot of the principles of persuasive communication and rhetoric through training with the Fusion Group in Florida. Unique in their framework for crafting and delivering effective communication, Fusion derives its name from the kind of messaging that gives an audience that special experience during which its connection with the speaker generates a release of energy. Organizing communication into threes feels right. Fusing together mind, body, and spirit makes all the difference. So don't fight the feeling. When you need to say something—or play the sixteenth hole at the Downs—recall the symmetry of threes.

8

Lofty and Low

Describing the seventeenth hole as lofty and low only begins to capture one of the zaniest, most unusual holes classical golf architecture will ever know. Alfred E. Neumann of *Mad* magazine, toking Jamaica's finest, could not have created a more original design. A longer and wilder version of its shorter sister the eleventh that it parallels. The seventeenth hole requires golfers to tee off from high ground, bounce the shot off a significant depression, and hope the second shot puts them back on an infinitely high and wildly tilted putting surface. Picture in your mind a roller coaster called *Uber Hades* and you begin to get the idea.

Lofty and low sits next to the philosophical construct of yin and yang. Yin and yang convey the power of opposites, the tension between light and dark, high and low, male and female. Lofty and low takes this ancient dynamic to a new level.

Yin and yang infuse your thinking as you ponder which club to use from the tee. If you try to overpower the hole and its huge hill with your driver, you risk a second shot with a tough stance or a tough lie in the tall fescue that surrounds the green—or both. If you opt to lay up low and just over the deep cavern, you need to "eye-drop" your second shot onto the same elevated green—from way below. If neither of these unappetizing options appeal to you, you do what most average golfers attempt. You pound it into the hill to no avail, yin yanging your way to a new understanding. Don't try to overpower or *over finesse*. Hit a solid tee ball to a hundred yards and then hit your best wedge—with quiet legs. A little bit of yang and a lot of yin.

Such *finesse* also characterizes great communication. Holding opposing ideas in our mind rationally leads to persuasion. Aristotle called it pro/con; Ben Franklin used his T chart. Persuasion starts in the brain of your audience members. From their mind-set, you can bring them, step by step, to a new perspective. Think of how much more compelling an argument becomes when we present a high-minded idea in basic terms, when we tackle the mighty with the mundane— truly lofty and low. History can be marked by this kind of enlightened persuasion. Imagine standing up to the tyranny and terror of Adolf Hitler with a garden hose. Seem too ridiculous to imagine? Well, that's exactly what President Franklin D. Roosevelt did in one of his most famous and effective fireside chats.

In 1940, Adolf Hitler bestrode most of continental Europe. Absorbing the Czech Republic and Austria, defeating Poland and France in short order, Herr Hitler readied himself for a cross-channel invasion of England. The Low Countries provided the launching grounds he needed for his Luftwaffe-protected ground forces to hurdle the English Channel and spread his terror to London and the rest of the Kingdom. FDR knew the math.

Keeping England and Russia in the war meant providing both with the food, guns, ammunition, and the military hardware they needed to stave off invasion. Hence, Roosevelt created the Lend–Lease Act—and the metaphor of the garden hose to help sell it to the American people. Talk about low!

As he explained in his broadcast on December 11, 1940, Europe was our neighbor. If our neighbor's kitchen caught on fire, we would naturally want to help before the blaze took over the whole house and spread to ours. So, what do we do? We lend our neighbor our garden hose. We don't sell it or rent it. We lend it—only expecting it to be returned to us in good working order after the fire.

Great American battleships entered the war under British command—the USS *Alabama* became the *HMS Black Knight*. Britain stayed in the war and survived. The British, along with the Russians, did a lot of fighting for us—fighting for which they paid dearly. Meanwhile, we began to build the factories to supply them and keep them fighting. Later, when the outcome began to take shape, America would claim the prize. We were then ready to be a superpower. Did we help stop Hitler? You bet. Did we lessen our own losses while our friends suffered more heavily? You bet. Did we build up our own economy while helping to destroy our competitors? Of course. Did we ready ourselves for world rule? Absolutely! FDR took lofty and low to a whole new level.

Lofty and low came quite naturally to my dad; to his dad, Donnell; and to his son, Kirk. Grandpa Don found Downriver Detroit when he escaped from Ohio as a teenage runaway. It's the low ground of Detroit in more ways than one. Full of factories, rail yards, and docks, it's always been low on the list of Detroit's high culture spots, but high on the enemy's target list. Truly, the Downriver earned its tag as the "Arsenal of Democracy."

Married there, Donnell and his wife welcomed a son, Donny, who arrived on a cold March evening at Wyandotte General Hospital. Twenty years later, President Eisenhower penned him a thank-you note for rounding up votes efficiently in the 1952 presidential election. When Donny crossed the Ann Arbor Law School Quadrangle on the way to his graduation, father and son completed their own journey together from low to lofty.

Donny loved the seventeenth hole. It seemed almost unimaginable, much like his own journey. He also greatly admired FDR and his ability to persuade, communicate, and lead. Persuasion came naturally to Donny. Lofty and low. That lens affected his vision in life. It perfected it—like his beloved seventeen.

9

Clearing

My dad may have been a tad too smart for this world. "Dad, don't I want to hit a high draw like Snead? Maybe a trap cut like Jack?" Donny asked gently, "What's wrong with straight?"

He reasoned that if the ball traveled only a certain distance, why not all in the direction that you intend? Intention—or, better yet, pure intention—seemed like Dad's inner mantra. He might focus on the wrong thing sometimes, but pure intention remained his special gift. Plus, he hoped I would strike a golf ball better than he did, which is what most golfers want for their kids.

Standing way up high on the eighteenth tee, straight works. You've now cleared the woods and forest of holes eleven through seventeen. You're now completely out in the open. Crystal Lake dominates the southern and eastern horizons. The majesty of the big lake consumes the long western horizon, right into the sunset. You're clear. The hole stretches diagonally from short left to long right, far below as you stand on a hillside of tall fescue grass—a blond fescue almost blown dry by the steady breeze off the lake. Decide how much tall fescue you intend to clear and hit it straight. Like the tee ball on the tenth *Sir Isaac Newton and the guy upstairs take care of the rest.*

In the field of behavioral psychology, the concept of clearing away the charged trauma of the past seems pretty straightforward. Revisit the memory. Relive it more vividly in your mind, with your own words. Rinse and repeat. Rinse and repeat. Shorten the length of the traumatic event. Rinse and repeat. Repeat and shorten it enough and it will pop. How do you know? You might chuckle or giggle or laugh—mostly at yourself. It all starts with intention. You have to want it. You have to want to let it all go.

How do you know when you're clear? The chuckle or giggle—or whatever brings about your awareness of your own traumatized humanity—is an early sign of letting go of the past. Then you begin to notice the absence of imagery and emotional impulses inside yourself when hit with a traumatic trigger—a decrease in the mind's tendency to jump from one awful memory to the next. (In Asia, they call it the "monkey mind.") When you've accepted that something horrible has happened, and become fully aware that the emotions and visceral feelings you actually sense no longer apply to your life *now*—what's past is past—you actually feel your mind empty itself of that old, charged pulse. You relax. Your shoulders might drop. Your breath might steady. After a while, you notice that you feel clear—not impelled to feel or do anything other than what you intend. That's the new source of energy from deep inside, where love resides.

A thirteen-year-old boy should know right from wrong. Yet, when a twenty-three year-old fill-in babysitter sits herself next to a teenage boy, it can be hard to resist and do the right thing. As she coyly nudged at my side, she created exactly the reaction she wanted. Using her hand to find her way underneath my blue jeans, my reaction was natural and premature—on many levels. What wasn't natural was her laughter and scorn. As if it was *my* response that constituted the transgression. What could have been a moment of vulnerability and playfulness became fused with embarrassment and shame.

Not the way it's supposed to be. Her accusations silenced me, burrowing my shame into a deep bunker.

What happens between a man and a woman should be difficult to describe. After all, every culture devotes a significant amount of ceremony and ritual as a preamble to the intimacy that will occur between them. What makes this event very simple is the sensation of joy and rapture reserved for this sacred act of giving and receiving. Cascading beyond merely the physical, it's the ultimate act of pure evolutionary fusion: mind, body, and spirit. What a difference from my thirteen-year-old experience! To enjoy the beauty of a woman without impulse—or, even worse, compulsion. No longer do I drag myself down with the memory of that babysitter luring me into a lousy version of sex. I now know that keeping the abuse a secret allowed me to bury it into an emotional bunker—a bunker sodded over by forty years of dirty jokes and sexual stories meant to demean its malevolent and troubled perpetrator. Like I was fooling myself, or anyone else.

With the support of a professional, my old memory file was held up to the light of current day. Held up at a healthy distance. Over and over, I restated out loud what happened. "Again, please. Shorten it up this time." After I revisited it over and over and over, it finally "popped." It released. It subsided. I was then able to chuckle and, eventually, laugh at myself: a thirteen-year-old boy doing something I knew little about— and doing it very poorly. Not bad, kid. Not bad. But not love. The eighteenth finishes with a nice sense of relief. Hard earned peace belongs to you. The uphill second shot is far easier than the second into the seventeenth, and you finish the final hole in an open space—a clearing of your own making as you walk off the course.

Sophrosyne

Clearing away the charged memories, traumas both micro and macro, and all those damn buttonwood trees provides a new, much more expansive view of life. The Greeks created a word for such a state of balanced serenity absent the pulse of hubris. *Sophrosyne* is soundness of mind and excellence of character. It's peace and freedom from one's charged-up past. It's perspective. That last hole at Crystal provides a metaphoric high ground for such a long view of life—a promontory. Now, let's tidy up a few loose ends.

Mom's Experimental Cooking

Mom put time, effort, and research into the meals she prepared for her family. Inheriting an elastic blood sugar chemistry from her mother's side, Mom threw away the thyroid pills in 1966 and started on a food regimen without refined sugar, grains, or the dreaded high-fructose corn syrup. Adele Davis was her nutritional madrina. Those early years were a little rough. Moving from copious amounts of pure white sugar and Crisco to plates of lean meat and fresh veggies required a little adjustment. All of us benefited, and eventually we took to similar fare for ourselves. I happily report that I still weigh twenty five pounds too much, but my cholesterol is one hundred plus my age, and my curly Black Irish locks now carry more than a hint of gray. Mom has never given up her vodka martinis with no vermouth, and a twist. Soon to be eighty-two she's still experimenting in the kitchen.

Joe Simpson

Joe lost the 1989 US Senior Amateur to Bo Williams during the finals at Lochinvar in Houston. Joe played a lot of very fine golf during his amateur career. His greater accomplishment, however, may have been to bring along his son, Scott, who won the '87 U.S. Open at Olympic. Scott also played on Walker and Ryder Cup teams, and won the Champions Tour title in 2006. To win that Open at Olympic, Scott birdied fourteen, fifteen, and sixteen to overtake Tom Watson (the pro whose swing I tried to copy) and win with a tournament score of 276. Second place was 277. Seems like Joe accomplished quite a bit.

Limping Windshield Wiper

Ethical dilemmas come in all shapes and sizes. Does Donnell volunteer to the police that the windshield wiper needed to be serviced? Does he risk the police and the victim's family focusing on the wiper and minimizing the other factors? Does he risk being charged or sued by a family with very little means—a family who didn't even bother to show up at the burial? You would like to think that Grandpa Don would demonstrate the strength of character to do the right thing. What was the "right" thing?

Had he volunteered the information to the police, he might have been charged. He might have been subject to a trial or lengthy investigation. His seventeen-year-old son would surely have been called to testify or would have been subject to some fairly grueling interrogations. After all, his son was driving the car that ran over and killed the victim. If Donnell had been charged and convicted, would his son be in better shape? Or worse? All these questions undoubtedly hung over Grandpa and his family during this period. I'm told Grandma was not exactly a pillar of strength during this trauma. She seemed more intent on protecting the family reputation than on providing comfort to her son and husband. Not her finest hour, as we've heard from family and friends. I shudder to imagine the guilt Donny would have carried if his beloved father had gone to jail for an act he committed. Maybe it's no wonder that he went to law school. Dad served his penance at that Law Quad in Ann Arbor.

In the end, neither my dad nor Grandpa Donnell shared with the police that the windshield wiper needed servicing. In their minds, it hadn't gotten drunk and staggered into a six-lane highway. It was the poor, troubled man—with his own set of deep emotional bunkers—who found his way onto that rainy, foggy highway that night.

The Ugly Babysitter

Legendary basketball coach John Wooden used to say, "Everyone is my teacher. I can learn what to do. I can learn what not to do." I put my babysitter in that category. She taught me what not to do.

Mental health professionals suggest that most episodes that carry a "charge" in the recesses of one's mind relate either to sex or death. After I became aware of my own experience, I've been able to view others through a lens that is much more clear.

It's likely that this babysitter carried her own set of charges related to sex, maybe from a young age. Typically, girls and women are on the receiving end of this kind of behavior. However, we need only think back to the Catholic Church or the Penn State scandal to know that boys are also, and all too often, subject to the misconduct of damaged adults. It all starts somewhere. Who knows what that babysitter endured in her own life? However, if there were any abuses in her past, I stopped the cycle. I made a different choice.

With empathy, sophrosyne can begin to quell our charged impulses. As the charges lighten, hubris—a disconnect from reality and an overestimation of one's competence or capabilities—also begins to disappear. My dad exhibited hubris as an investor, particularly as a real estate investment sponsor. He showed a knack for making good deals, building

Kirk D. Dodge

on budget and on time, and then managing the properties profitably. Why, then, did he get out into the skinny branches? Putting together a series of funds and providing overall asset management seemed a bit much, particularly for an attorney without a background in finance and management.

Grandpa Donnell seemed to live a life much closer to this ideal of sophrosyne. He possessed only a sixth-grade education, and he seemed to know his limits. Maybe that's the key ingredient for most of us: operating within our limits, avoiding the skinny branches, and seeing ourselves through a realistic and loving lens.

— 42 —

— PART II —

FRONT NINE: Adult Mind of a Teacher

Begin with the End in Mind

Learning new concepts and ideas late in life can fundamentally alter your perspective. As I began the process of revisiting difficult and embarrassing episodes from my youth, a certain rationality and evenhanded mindset began to emerge. Holding up for examination memory files fused by shame into guilt requires seeing events from more than one perspective.

For centuries, great minds have asserted the virtue of holding two opposing ideas in your mind at the same time. Ancient Asian teachings suggest a yin and yang to all things. Aristotle described the pro/con method of persuasion. Ben Franklin laid out his T chart of positives and negatives. F. Scott Fitzgerald praised those that could hold two competing ideas in mind at the same time and still function effectively. Rationality requires the ability to hold difficult conflicts within our minds at a healthy distance, and unravel the considerations and assessments we bring to such events. From these conflicts, our insights emerge. This tension lays the predicate for progress.

My anthology of stories and essays surface the concepts around learning to see the world, and, your own world, more clearly and rationally. This journey makes numerous stops

along the way. Memories flow from mother and father to early gifts of books, sports and holidays. It includes childhood jobs, schoolwork and career endeavors.

Swimming from well spent and misspent youth, this journey connects the boulders and waterholes between those younger days, adulthood and the sunset of life. A journey that endeavors to perfect the art of reason and sophrosyne. Greeks used this word sophrosyne to describe a personal journey without hubris, and the mask of excess pride. A journey that never ends. A journey that nourishes life.

Crystal Downs is a wonderful old golf course. As a young boy, it provided the backdrop to a series of tender memories. In these stories, it serves as metaphor. Both crystal clear and from the "downs" of life, it provides texture to the highs and lows. Accepting both these ups and downs makes all the difference.

For me, this openness of mind seems quite liberating. It allows me to perfect the art of living, while accepting that life itself can never be perfect.

Only the journey can perfect us.

These stories and tales become the water of life. They hydrate the heart. They wash over us. In the end, they cleanse us.

11

Blue Hour

Twice a day, every day, light and dark tussle for dominance. Sunrise and sunset paint a blue hour where neither can claim victory or defeat. My first day of life included a sunset, a sunrise and another sunset as I overstayed my welcome inside my mother's birth canal. It took 22 hours to travel from that peaceful, serene and dark womb to the bright, noisy maternity ward of Wyandotte General Hospital. It's said that life reveals its tough, arduous eternal lessons handed down through centuries of Scripture. "That which doesn't kill us, makes us stronger". This was true for mother as it was for me. Despite high forceps and an inexperienced resident obstetrician during the first 20 hours, it didn't kill her or me. More importantly, maybe just maybe, it made us stronger. It took nearly a full day for the two of us to claim the victory of life.

The very first hole at Crystal Downs offers two powerful versions of this "blue hour". Opalescent blue dawn can be viewed to the east as light permeates the atmosphere. This beauty beguiles our heart. Standing on the first tee at dawn you absorb a full dose of this morning profusion of fractured waves. At sunset, looking west, the scattering of light and dark radiates even more intensely blue as it passes through the moisture evaporating off the Big Lake. I ache for that blue hour with my father. My mother gave me life. My father made it worth living.

This first hole at Alister Mackenzie's Crystal Downs challenges golfers with an arduous, seemingly interminable downhill and then uphill opening par four. This first hole at Crystal is wondrously expansive and long, requiring two very strong, well struck shots. Then the real trouble begins. The putting surface itself steepens and gives you pause. If you have left yourself a downhill putt or end up on the right side of the green forget about it. Gravity will punish you with your next shot being a chip to return to this dastardly surface. As an opening hole greeting the golfer, this is a very, very firm handshake.

Crystal Downs may be the most difficult and robust golf course that is not overly long or overly narrow. Alister Mackenzie simply mastered the challenge of making each and every yard, a changing surface that requires concentration of mind and steady balance from the body. With ground that undulates constantly under your feet, bring your A game. As

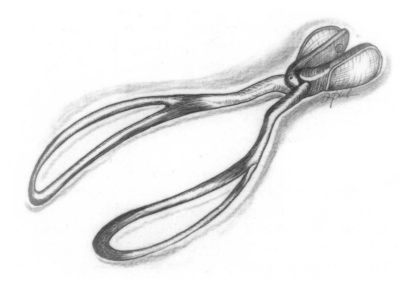

life frequently shifts under our feet, so too does this hallowed golf design artistically spread across the isthmus between Lake Michigan and its ancient bay, Crystal Lake.

"God creates great golf courses—the architect simply reveals them…". Attributed to a number of legendary classic golf architects, this concept parallels the process by which adults come to a clear, uncharged view of their own mind, body and spirit. Revealing to ourselves that which hasn't killed us, that which makes us stronger. Letting go requires exposing to ourselves those tough, painful, sometimes traumatic memories sodded over by years of shame and denial. This clearing process requires repeated "visits". It also requires forgiving… mostly oneself. Chuckling at our own flawed past, we let ourselves "off the hook". Most importantly, these painful revisits lead to a clear, more restive peace of mind. A pure blue hour where light ~ dark, good ~ evil, positive ~ negative find a full resolve.

"Blue hour" inspires writers, poets, musicians and painters with its beautiful fracturing of light across the prism of color. Even car designers get it. My first half dozen cars all scattered blue light off the fenders and rocker panels. The interiors warmed my senses with sunshine yellows, caramels and tans. Hanging in my closet, I choose from a range of blue suits and tweed, many with the occasional fleck or plaid of saddle cream and beige. I own far too many blue shirts and yellow ties.

My early years of twilight golf with a generous father imprinted me with this rather understated, but narrow color palette. During dad's early years of golf, he probably played more than enough hard, opening golf holes at Barton Hills, Grosse Ile and the University of Michigan course in Ann Arbor. Maybe being with *his* son at Crystal Downs provided *me* a gift of something more important. Sporting his blue eyes and sandy brown hair, walking memories of my father on his beloved Crystal Downs reveals to me that being tough means much more than not crying and feeling. It's knowing that those moist tears of remembrance can wash away life's dirt and grime. They can clear away the path to pain. Becoming strong enough to fully feel and weep can actually help end the tears, and blue the sky of our future.

A bountiful blue hour, we find within ourselves. A place of sensory acuity which allows us to fully experience the world around us. As we let go of "reasons", "blame" and "fault", our mind clears of charged impulses and racing thoughts. This clearness of mind ~ body ~ spirit brings a sensitivity and awareness that lays the predicate for learning and education. This is a process that forms the second phase, the second hole on the front nine of life.

12

Reading to Decode

When your mother makes her living teaching young children their alphabet, cursive letters and sounds, reading no longer becomes an option. If you want to eat, you learn to read. Her first gifts to me included biographies of sports heroes and political figures. For some reason, the most impactful gift detailed the lives and accomplishments of Abigail and John Adams, our second President of "these states united" and the love of his life, his wife of 54 years. Sometimes, what comes second can be even better than what comes first.

The second hole at Crystal Downs comprises the yin to the yang of #1. It is a mirror image, but slightly shorter and all uphill and a natural opposite of its companion first. It's a wee bit wider, curvier and more voluptuous than its male partner. It's the Abigail to John. Not to be trifled with, and you better respect her. From the tee box, #2 seems so benign. It rises in front of you. It's gentle. On the surface, it appears almost mellow. Mining the right side lays the same deep gnarly bunker that seems so imposing from the opening box on #1. Here this very same bunker teases you into ignoring it. That's a profound mistake. She can look sweet. However, for the player who fails to respect her properly, you'll face an uphill shot over a rising face and more trouble looms along the right. If you fail to make a smooth swing with even tempo, flairs to the right find only tall fescue grass.

Trouble makes trouble, and the trouble trouble makes, makes more trouble. Any husband who fails to show his wife the proper respect knows exactly how this feels.

Abigail Adams may have been a teenage bride without a formal education, but she brought to her marriage one huge advantage. She read damn near every book in some of the finest libraries of Colonial Massachusetts. Self taught by reading the classics, she kept her Harvard educated husband on his toes. Most importantly, John loved her for it. Their communication achieved the lofty and lovely reserved for two well read and intense lovers. Their 1,160 existing letters kept in the archives at Harvard provide a window to their incandescent romance.

Margaret A. Hogan is Managing Editor of the Adams Papers at the Massachusetts Historical Society and Co-editor with C. James Taylor of *My Dearest Friend: Letters of Abigail and John Adams*. She writes:

Abigail found writing to John "the composure of my mind." John, even more strikingly, asked, "Is there no Way for two friendly Souls, to converse together, although the Bodies are 400 Miles off?—Yes by Letter.—But I want a better Communication. I want to hear you think, or see your Thoughts. The Conclusion of your Letter makes my Heart throb, more than a Cannonade would. You bid me burn your Letters. But I must forget you first.

Can two seemingly reserved New England intellectuals share so much passion and romantic love, love marked by mutual respect and admiration? Much like the underestimated #2 at Crystal Downs, don't judge a book by its cover. Particularly, when the subject includes two souls so capable of elocution and intimacy. While these two personages now frame the second Presidency of the United States, in the late 1700's they were merely a young married couple enthralled with other.

Again from Margaret Hogan: "Miss Adorable," John wrote. "By the same Token that the Bearer hereof sat up with you last night I hereby order you to give him, as many Kisses, and as many Hours of your Company after 9 O Clock as he shall please to Demand and charge them to my Account." In time their flirtatious correspondence evolved to reflect a deeper, more abiding relationship, but they never lost what Abigail described as "that unabated affection which has for years past, and will whilst the vital spark lasts, burn in the Bosom of your affectionate A Adams."

When the members at Crystal Downs finally reach their wide and luscious #2 putting green, they face a two putt that requires extra close study. The subtle break of the ground from right to left and back to front can be indiscernible to the casual eye. Much like a marriage partner that deserves our close listening, this green requires careful attention. If you can two putt #2, be happy that you decoded this subtle terrain. Climb to the #3 tee box with some sweet satisfaction.

13

Taking Ground

Jumping on my orange Schwinn banana seat bike, throwing the canvas bag over my shoulder with the day's edition of the "Freeport News", and delivering newspapers could be made better only by one thing. Signing up another home to a new subscription…that felt great! It's said that sales people are born to sell. I'm not so sure. You have to overcome inertia. Step away from the television. Sign up to be a newspaper deliverer. Pick up the newspapers after school. Hop on a bike.

Pedal. And deliver. And, once in awhile, not every day, you sign up another subscriber, another house. "Taking ground" meant expanding your route. New houses, new streets was my start in sales. "Taking what the ground gives you" became an early lesson in how to sell on a number of levels.

Few holes in golf take the terrain that's given like the par 3 third hole at the Downs. If Alister Mackenzie mastered the art of crafting holes into the ground the good Lord gave him, #3 fits perfectly. Making the climb from the fecund surfaces of #2, the terrain begins to open under you. Taking in with your eye what #3 offers includes seeing down this medium short hole and into its ground. Dune grass forms a high back wall softened by two sand bunkers disassembling into the slope. The green angles gently from front right to back left as your mind tries to calculate the true distance. The terrain tricks the eye. It's lower than you think. A ball traveling 180 yards in the air seems to land softly. As if you dropped the ball from above, the slope absorbs its momentum. Still, too much club or too much force and the ground penalizes you with rear sand flowing up the slope into the woods. Like in sales, you cannot force it. You take what's given.

The question becomes how do you know what's given? How do you know what's enough? What's too much? The answer lies within. The answer lies in the question. From the questions we ask, the answers emerge.

"Mrs. Johnstone, how do you stay in touch with family and friends back home?" "Do you read about it?" "Send them news from here?" "How do you keep up with news here in Freeport?" "Word of mouth?" "How is your tv reception? Radio?" "Hope it's better than ours…"

Conversational questions, gently offered and a relationship builds. The sale simply emerges. No force required. You're letting them in on a little secret. They just bought something, another subscription to the "Freeport News". Another subscriber, maybe two if the family back home wants one—another house on another street. You're taking ground, one by one. You're taking what the ground gives you. Sales seemed so noble to me.

Nothing forced, always by consent. Young people begin creating agreements. I deliver your newspaper. You buy a subscription. I deliver on time. You pay on time. If there is a problem, I come tell you about it. I'm accountable to you. You're accountable to me. Commerce begins and our web of goodness expands, home by home, street by street. One more young person starts down the path to adulthood. Taking what the ground gives them.

14

Abnegation

When you're nine like I was, living on an isolated island, like I was, playmates and buddies can seem few and far between. You might just fall in with older kids. Sometimes, they're a girl. Jan Nunley was a full year older and a bit of a tomboy. An old fashioned word used to describe girls who played the same games as boys. Tomboys could seem "bossy", or maybe they just had leadership skills. Jan brought all of the above to our budding little friendship.

Grand Bahama Island experienced a mini-boom in the late 1960's. Construction trucks filled the lots where homes and condominiums sprouted up like spring flowers. Every time you looked around, another project would start. Jan liked playing in the unfinished homes. In fact, she liked to play "house" in the unbuilt homes. She wasn't "bossy", she just had leadership skills. She would have made an imposing wife and mother.

Standing on the fourth tee at Crystal Downs, you can barely see around the bend. You cannot fully see past the corner. You're "blind" to the second half of the golf hole as it slopes up to its putting green and pin. A large bunker guards the right side of the hole and the corner. It's tempting to try to clear it with your drive. It's doable. It's also chancy as a miss to the right takes you into a large stand of trees that follow the entire right side of the hole. Staying left would be the smart play. Less risk, and the hole opens up visually and with a better angle to the green, if you hit your ball down the left side. As in life, the temptations can be hard to resist.

Jan wore white canvas tennis shoes with white socks. Wrapped stacks of lumber and bags of nails lay strewn about the floors and staircases of these unfinished homes. Sometimes, the bags would lay open and nails would scatter around the floor. I noticed them. I even mentioned them to Jan. She ignored me. She ignored the nails. One day, as she showed me our "dining room" with her hands gesturing and pointing, she yelped and grimaced in pain. I noticed her right tennis shoe no longer looked white and bright. It filled with red and very dark blood.

Sure enough, despite my warning her, she stepped onto a couple nails which popped through her shoe and sock and she couldn't stop the bleeding. No more playing "house". She hobbled home, trying not to lean too hard on my shoulder as she walked. Once home, we both endured a parental interrogation and a litany of reminders as to why we'd been told not to play on these construction sites. Accusatory questions hit us hard. It was as if *I had done something wrong*.

Both sets of parents took us to our pediatrician's office and both of us received penicillin shots to prevent any infection. Just a day or two apart, we received the same type of shot. Mine went fine. Hers didn't go well. My staff infection never developed. Hers did.

Within a month, she developed aplastic anemia. Within six months, she died.

The second half of the fourth hole seems much more daunting than the beginning. It's uphill. It's partly blind to the putting green. Surrounding it, coffin size bunkers mine the rear and right hand hillside. It's menacing to the eye. It's worse on the actual green.

No matter how hard you stroke an uphill putt, it's probably not enough. Sometimes, as in life, it can actually be harder and tougher than it looks.

My mother sat me down to tell me Jan would not be returning from the hospital. She struggled for a couple days with how to tell me. She knew I'd hear from our neighbors. Everyone felt awkward. The moms felt it the most. Few of the mothers genuinely liked Jan. Those "leadership skills" made her a little hard to take. She could be a bit of a pain and nuisance to the moms. Now, they all felt a full measure of guilt. Mom knew all of this, and knew she needed to find the right words. There were no "right" words. She told me calmly and thoughtfully. I looked out the kitchen window. I stared at the unfinished home beyond our back fence. I stared and imagined my bossy little buddy telling me where our dining room table would be. I swallowed hard. I looked archly at my mom and asked, "What's for lunch?"

I didn't let Jan off the hook. I put myself there instead. An eleven year old boy trying a little too hard to be tough, tough like my dad, tough like my grandfather. It all became a grand effort, an abnegation.

The fourth hole is a toughie. Finishing it without losing your head can seem like an accomplishment. I didn't quite pull that off as a kid. I did better when I revisited this ground as an adult.

15

Lonely Ideas

My mother honored my ideas, even the "lonely" ones. She once described how as an undergraduate college student she had written a paper for a philosophy class. After turning it in, the professor found it hard to believe that an undergraduate, an underclassmen undergraduate, could produce such a trenchant, potent and creative essay. Convinced that she'd reproduced someone else's writing, he scanned titles in the University Library. He walked the "stacks" looking for a book or source which would confirm the plagiarism. No such luck, he could find no work that she copied or mimicked. Yet, he told her plainly, she couldn't have created it herself—simply not conceivable to him. He told her simply, you will not remain in this program. Choose to transfer or he'd make this unbearable for her. After a trip home for the weekend, she found little parental support. Fighting through it, it scarred her for life. It became a piece of baggage she carried the rest of her life.

So, she made it a point to never deny me my thoughts, my ideas and my dreams. She taught me that love started with honoring those that we love, even their "lonely" ideas. She found her own unique and authentic way to love me. She did it without exception.

A lonely oak tree dominates the view from the tee box on the fifth hole at the Downs. It's a lonely idea. Virtually every "expert" golf architect thinks it should be felled to the orthodoxy of timeless, classic golf course design. It's a lonely idea to keep it. It guards the right side of the hole. It "tells" you to keep your tee shot to the left. That tree communicates loudly, every time a golfer contemplates their first swing on the fifth hole. No need for a guidebook, this lonely tree provides expert guidance.

#5 provides Crystal Downs members a golf hole for all time. If you scan books that catalogue golf's greatest holes, invariably you will see the Downs #5. George Peper led Golf Magazine for many years and wrote multiple books on great golf architecture. His seminal work may be "The 500 Greatest Holes in Golf", updated in 2003. Sure enough, there you will see Crystal Downs #5. While every expert rails about the need to take down this iconic tree, there it stands in every photograph Lonely ideas carry potential currency because they're lonely. As a long time associate and owner at the Capital Group, I first learned about "lonely ideas" put to work on behalf of the many mutual funds within the American Funds family. Ideas that made all the difference for our advisors and their clients, our shareholders.

Many of our securities analysts and portfolio counselors could detail the potency of these lonely ideas. None could bring them to life better than the late Steve Bepler. "Sir Bep" to his buddies, Steve brought a strong countenance to his work. His leadership as a portfolio counselor included the "New Perspective Fund" and "Capital World Growth and Income". His finest work may have been "Fundamental Investors", where he led this stock picking and portfolio management group that the Morningstar rating firm named their "Managers of the Decade" in the year 2000.

Lonely ideas found their way into our portfolios on the recommendation of the analyst who covered that industry and its group of companies. Names like Time Warner, AOL, Intel and Cisco started as investment recommendations of analysts like Gordie Crawford and Jim Martin. They started as lonely ideas as each counselor enjoyed the latitude of deciding when and how much to own in the sleeve they managed.

In the automotive space, our analyst was Darcy Kopcho. Her talents extended beyond pure investment analysis. She actually created an economic and financial model which tracked key macroeconomic variables like employment, new automotive part orders, consumer loan rates and undelivered new car supply levels. She established that successful investing in a cyclical industry like autos required investing in the most attractive companies *at the most attractive low price points in the cycle*. Her work contributed to many successful investments like Toyota, BMW and, in the days after the August invasion of Kuwait in 1990, the Chrysler Corporation. No one pounced on this lonely and controversial Chrysler idea faster and more prolifically than "Sir Bep".

Steve overcame childhood polio. Smarter and tougher for overcoming his challenging and modest upbringing, he developed an ability to see the 360 degree nature of crisis and opportunity. In addition, his investment acuity often came camouflaged in a wry blend of insight and humor. The counter intuitive nature of seeing past the everyday to the "lonely idea" would often show up in his very sage observations. This was Steve at his best:

> "While fortune favors the brave, a fool and his money are soon parted."
> "The emperor never had any clothes after all; now we'll discover he didn't have any money either".

The invasion of Kuwait rocked the investment world as markets faced the prospect that Saddam Hussein could choke off the Straits of Hormuz and drive up the price of oil. Fear hit auto stocks especially hard with significant price drops. Chrysler dropped below $10 per share. In addition, the Chrysler Chairman Bob Eaton acknowledged that they didn't anticipate the Kuwait invasion, and they faced fierce rebating for their Jeeps and SUVs, while suffering from significant overcapacity as they converted to their new "cab forward" car designs. The bad "news" only mounted, as the media sold newspapers into the growing fears in the marketplace. Led by Steve, the Capital Group established in the fall of 1990 a 5.9% ownership interest in Chrysler at an average cost below $10 per share. This investment helped set a "floor" for the stock, and helped contribute to saving the company. Then, they rode the stock up to the $60 per share that Daimler Benz offered less than eight years later in May of 1998.

Our shareholders ranged from retirement plan participants in companies like Whirlpool and Trader Joe's to retirees with IRA rollovers and savings across middle class America. Senior portfolio counselors like Steve kept younger associates keenly aware that our assets did not represent, in fact, our money. They represented the sacred retirement nest eggs of millions of average Americans. No one championed the lonely ideas quite as Steve could. Fewer still chose to articulate their importance like the guy we knew as "Sir Bep".

It's said that we should remember that the number of buyers and sellers in the stock market everyday are always equal. The individual prices may rise and fall, but there is always someone on the other side of the trade. If you're a seller, there's a buyer on the other side. Despite this truism, the emotions of fear and greed can dominate our investment psyche. It takes professional skill to see past the headlines. However, skill must be backed up by a calm, cool and reasoned mindset. Smarts and skill need a willingness and comfort in standing alone. The guy we knew as "Sir Bep" delivered exactly that countenance when it really mattered. You could even say he was always a "polite" investor.

When people were desperate to sell, he would buy. When they were desperate to buy, he would sell.

Finally, when the cancer he'd conquered earlier in his life began to return, he didn't look inward. He looked generously towards young people that he could assist with his considerable wealth. Beyond his philanthropy in New York, and his alma mater Fordham University, he found the young students in the Lake Wales Charter School District, near his winter home in Florida. Despite the modest incomes in this area, these families and teachers had transformed their charter district into a high performer. As Steve listened to the students perform classical music and jazz, his eyes would moisten with the purity of their effort and accomplishment. His generous gifts led directly to these students of modest means gaining access to college and beyond. He expanded the web of goodness.

Using his skills and strong countenance, he made the world a better place than he found it.

His enormous strength stood tall without fanfare like that lonely tree of an idea on #5 at Crystal Downs. The remaining shot on that hole seems so much easier once you've transcended and passed that lonely tree. As in life, once we've stood tall and shown courage, life becomes easier.

16

Camoufleur

As we grow older, good financial fortune can open up new careers, new vistas where we can take our lives in a new direction. Careers can sometimes be camouflaged by our early choices. Ronald Reagan began as a radio announcer. Then, he left the Midwest for Hollywood where he appeared in a running string of uncritically acclaimed movies and television shows. Television and the GE Theatre brought him inside General Electric where he traveled across everyday America speaking to their factory workers. In turn, his speaking style won him a political following. This following led him to the Governor's mansion in Sacramento and, eventually, the White House.

Leaving behind a career as a salesman and marketing manager, I took my public speaking and writing skills to a remote school district in Central Florida. Teaching oration at the Bok Academy led to instructing from the autobiography of Edward W. Bok. A summer reading program included 27 eighth graders reading out loud, word by word, the autobiography of Jackie Robinson. Listening to young people tackle unfamiliar words with pure and genuine effort began to open my heart. These kids give more back to me, much more, than I give them. Writing about the experiences that formed the camouflage of my first 57 years seemed a natural next step.

Standing on the sixth tee at the Downs can present some confusing visual cues.

Similar to life, the proper direction can seem a bit of a mystery. A randomly shaped bunker marks a sloping hill guarding the right side and a tree just above it. The top of the pin flag behind that hill pulls it closer in your vision than reality. A steep hill on the other side remains blind along with the left to right movement of that hidden fairway. All camouflaged to trick your eye by none other than Dr. Alister Mackenzie, the architect who took the original nine hole course and turned them into an eighteen hole masterpiece.

Born to Scottish parents in 1870 near Lochinver, England, the good doctor began his professional life as a medical doctor. In fact, upon finishing his medical training at Cambridge, he served as a British Army field surgeon for the Territorial Unit of the Somerset Light Infantry in South Africa during the Boer War. On those remote battlefields, he learned about the art of camouflage and entrenchment, and their importance as tactics for tricking the eye. Scotoma afflicts golfers too, and the good doctor took clear advantage of the tendency of the mind to see what it wants to see.

Raised in Northern England, and born a Scot, Alister came to golf quite naturally. Serving as both a club captain (similar to a U.S. club president) and Chair of the Green Committee for the Alwoodley Golf Club, the good doctor couldn't help but connect what he learned about field camouflage to the subtleties of golf course design. Just as being a army field doctor led to camouflage, at age 49, Dr. Mackenzie decided to concentrate on his budding work as a golf architect. It would become a canvas that the world would come to revere and admire. Divorcing his wife of twenty-six years Edith Wedderburn, led to a new American life with his second wife Hilda Sykes Haddock. Young Alister became a newly open, wiser and more expansive Alister. Your drive on number six at Crystal requires you to be over the hill. Just as in life, being "over the hill" can, sometimes, open up vistas you couldn't previously see or imagine.

Hitting it over the hill on #6 gives you a second shot that's fairly short into a large green. It does not appear too daunting. When you get a close-up look at the green you see some very large slopes which con you with their furtive and stealthy breaks. Training as a code breaker or camoufleur would be handy. Two shots on and an unpleasant three putt happens every day on #6. A few gray hairs and wisdom becomes useful as you contemplate life after you're "over the hill". It's also useful as you try to make par on #6.

In a world where centuries of economic life meant working a subsistence living as a farmer or laborer, second careers can seem a modern indulgence and luxury. Most of human existence meant much of humanity could only calculate how much acreage would be needed to simply eat. How to grow sufficient food crops, graze livestock and provide the basic needs of a family.

Included among those bands of subsistence farmers living along the sea coasts would be sheep herders grazing their animals. With prime soil and fields reserved for wheat, rye, corn and beans, shepherdesses funneled their sheep past the sand blowouts and fallow meadows between the farms and the sea. These rolling pastures of grass and sand fed the sheep, and in turn their owners. It's written that golf sprouted as a game among these shepherds. Hitting sheep dung with their crooks seemed a harmless way to pass the boredom of following the sheep through the grassy lea and trying to avoid a messy misstep. Little did these poor Scots realize they invented a game that would someday captivate and frustrate centuries of modern citizens, particularly those retiring to central Florida.

To the Scots, this rolling land between the farms and the dunes next to the sea became known as "downs land". Not directly adjacent to the beach, these open meadows offered the pine, birch and scrubby trees the sandy soil they loved.

When 59 year old Alister Mackenzie saw, for the first time, the land we now know as "Crystal Downs", he was said to have declared "downs land…in the middle of the America!"

Nestled adjacent to the sandy bluffs above Lake Michigan and just south of the Sleeping Bear National Lakeshore, Crystal Downs charms its first time visitors. You expect such terrain on New York's Long Island or Cape Cod. Here it lies, just left of the knuckle of the pinky finger on the open right hand "Mitt" of Michigan. Truly, it's hallowed ground. Camouflaged by its Great Lakes location and the skill of Dr. Mackenzie, playing his design moves the spirit.

17

Hidden Treasure

Beginning with my father's sharp glance and hands gripped together in a sweeping motion, I understood his earliest silent invitations to play golf at Crystal Downs. The very words "Crystal" and "the Downs" conjure up sweet notions of natural landscape and warm emotions. Twenty years later, the late 1980's coincided with the emergence of the Downs as a notable place for the ancient game of golf. Literally, most of the years of the club's existence, the golf world barely knew that Alister Mackenzie applied his skills to a natural setting so well suited to the artistry of landscape architecture. Owing to its remote location and quiet reputation, the Club lacked the resources to alter the course. This shortage of capital literally prevented decades of green committees from screwing up this masterpiece.

Then, Ben Crenshaw came by for a visit. "Gentle Ben" Crenshaw won his first Masters Tournament in 1984 on the back of some of the best championship putting and short game that Augusta National ever witnessed. Soon after this major win, the young and talented golf architect Tom Doak invited Crenshaw to the Downs to apply his prodigious putting skills to its fiendish Mackenzie greens. Crenshaw was completely won over by this northernmost expression of the golf artistry that made Augusta National and the Masters Tournament so iconic. Crenshaw typically keeps his opinions in check. Within a few hours that day, he could hardly hold back his lavish praise for their design.

Just as the Downs remained for decades a hidden treasure, so does the hidden nature of the putting green on its seductive par four #7. Yes, that putting surface coyly wraps around the back of that ample green side bunker.

The seventh hole sets up with a shortened fairway that requires choosing the right club at the tee box. Hit your drive too far and the terrain punishes you with a tough downhill stance. Hitting from a downhill stance to an uphill green (with a shrouded back half) can fairly be described as among the

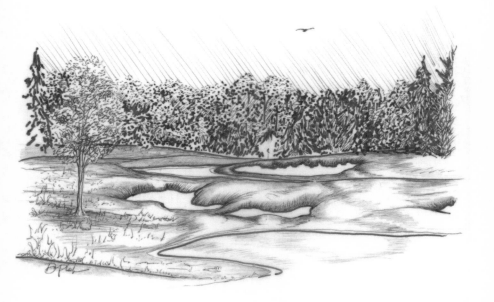

most difficult shots in golf. Dad loved the challenge. Relieved that I didn't storm off the course in frustration, he wanted his son to embrace what seemed too difficult and trying. The hidden nature of the back half of the green just added another layer to the cake. Just when you think you've finished, there is more...much more.

Persevering through a task seemingly too tough at first, can be a useful way of understanding who is likely to succeed in life. Some folks have grit, and lots of it. Contrast those, with people who just leg it out without genuine determination and repeated effort.

Consider this list of people with hidden talents and skills:

- George Washington lost five straight battles. He won the last couple, the ones that mattered.
- Marie Curie educated herself at the hidden "Floating University" in 19th century Poland.
- Franklin D. Roosevelt suffered polio and was forgotten until elected U.S. President four times.
- Margaret Thatcher ridiculed by her peers became Great Britain's first woman Prime Minister.
- Abe Lincoln lost eight elections until he won the Presidency and saved the Union.
- Tom Brady overlooked in the 2000 NFL Draft, Brady was selected with pick #199, a compensatory pick, in the sixth round, and has become one of, if not the greatest quarterback of all time.
- Katherine Johnson overcame racial prejudice to save NASA missions with her math brilliance.
- Alan Turing cracked the German codes, defeated the Nazis and kept it secret his whole life.
- Admiral Ray Spruance was unknown until he replaced Adm. Halsey at the Battle of Midway.
- Margaret Hamilton wrote the NASA computer code that saved the Apollo 11 moon mission.

Hidden talents dominate the high points of history. Does a relationship exist between "lonely ideas" and the idea of hidden talents and treasure? People who counter the obvious with original thinking applied away from public view and the court of public opinion.

The British smugly dismissed General George Washington as a mere "Colonialist", part of the rabble in this wild wilderness of the New World. After losing in Massachusetts and New York, he kept his freezing army together for the Christmas Eve crossing of the Trenton River. He won his first and most pivotal battle of the Revolutionary War.

19th century Poland lived under the alternating dominion of Germany and Russia. Educating women was strictly forbidden. Marie Curie found her way to the "Floating University" which operated in hiding. She left Warsaw for Paris and eventually discovered radioactivity along with early methods for radiation as a treatment for disease.

Finally, in early World War II, the tide of war seemed strongly against America and her allies. The "star" American admiral in the Pacific, William F. "Bull" Halsey contracted the skin affliction known as shingles. His advice to his superiors, "choose Ray Spruance to replace me at Midway". A relative unknown, Spruance was thought a battleship man unsuited to the tactics required in an air and carrier battle like Midway. Cunning, smart and a careful risk taker, providence and his fine judgment turned "four Jap carriers into burning flotsam".

All of these figures eventually exhibited a hidden treasure trove of talents, skills and years of learning by trial and error. Like #7 at the Downs, take your time to study the landscape, learn from your failures, and don't dare give up the effort.

18

Heading Home

Fierce pride fuels my mom when describing her great grandmother and grandfather who emigrated from Denmark in the 1870's and settled near Crystal Downs in the small harbor town of Elberta, Michigan. Born in 1848, Anna Lawson had lived a young spinster's life in the village of Ketting, on the island of Ilse, off the Jutland peninsula that forms from the north of Germany. Anna remembered an older boy, Hans Bjornson and his brother Juergen. The brothers left Ketting to attend Navigational School in Hamburg. To avoid eventual conscription into the German Navy, they just kind of disappeared. Now, she was sailing to America to marry Hans. Marriage can reconstitute a life. She needed a new home.

The eighth looks like it goes nowhere. Standing on the tee box, you're not quite sure where the hole ends. The flag you see in the distance on the left actually flies on the ninth green. You almost don't know how to start.

The eighth hole actually bends to the right. It's over 540 yards and mostly uphill. It feels and plays more like 600 yards. Even with titanium drivers and modern golf balls, making it onto this saddle green in two shots involves considerable risk. Uneven stances abound. Ups and downs mark this long fairway. Distances seem more than the yardage indicates. Try landing a three wood shot on the hood of a '59 Cadillac from an uphill stance—tough to pull off even if you're really talented. If camouflage creates deception, the eighth looks beyond deceptive from the tee, from the fairway and on the green. Dr. Mackenzie also thought another coffin size bunker blind to your third shot on the back right of the green would help totally discombobulate you. It will, if you let it.

Now, imagine 23 year old Anna Lawson contemplating an arranged marriage proposal to Hans Bjornson, a man she vaguely knew, living in a remote part of a faraway land where they didn't speak Danish or even German. As with #8, she might not have known how to begin. What did she, in fact, know? Her mom died in childbirth when her youngest brother arrived. Life as the only stepdaughter to an indifferent and gruff father with a new wife made her wonder if this was all life had to offer. His insouciance injured her. Teaching the young children of Ketting their ABCs and completing her household chores to the satisfaction of a critical, remote stepmother made for long grey Danish days.

America and Michigan may have sounded far off, but for Anna it couldn't be worse than the cold thatch of roof and stone her father called home? It was well worth the risk. Countless days at her father's seaside shanty with his new wife would be a chilly life sentence. She accepted the proposal. She agreed to meet her future husband in Chicago, October of 1871.

Not knowing what the future holds soon became even more ambiguous and intimidating. A running series of fires in the City of Chicago that August and September caught wind and became the Great Chicago Fire of October, 8th 1871. Anna's arrival on October 6th took her to a hostel on Belmont Avenue, the hub of Swedes, Finns and Danes living on its north side. This section of Chicago lined its streets with timber and wooden sidewalks. The wood structures and buildings could be constructed cheaply from the stands of white pine, cedar and oak throughout nearby Wisconsin and Michigan. It would prove to be providentially unlucky building material for a city about to catch fire. The fabled Mrs. Leary's cow and stable originally stood only blocks away. Fate caught Anna in the wrong place at the wrong time.

Hans and his shipmates anchored their commercial schooner on Lake Erie near Buffalo when word arrived of the catastrophe happening at the western edge of the Great Lakes. Not enough time to set sail, he quickly arranged a train ticket and arrived in Chicago on October 12th to begin the search for his shy, resolute but unlucky bride.

As she lay asleep during her third night in Chicago, she picked up the odor of smoldering hay and dung from the horse stable across the street. Collecting her thoughts, she deduced the worst. Through the window, she could see the blaze coming from above the stable. She could hear the fire outside her door to the hall. Opening the door, she saw that flames laced the railing of the hall staircase and blocked her way from her room down the stairs. She had another escape route. She could climb through the window onto the steeply pitched porch roof over the burning sidewalk. Staring out the window, flames nipping at her favorite scarf that wrapped her head. Quickly, she made up her mind. Out the window she would go. With the scarf becoming very hot, she pushed on the mullion of the window with her open palm. The wooden mullions were too hot. She pushed on them with her open hands just long enough to force open the lower half of the window. With her scarf and hair catching the flame, she slipped through and onto the roof. With nothing to hold onto, she started to slide. Trying to plant her feet in the gutter along the bottom edge of the roof no luck, she slid down the steep roof and off into the street. With her hands flaying at her scarf, she managed to stop the burning feeling on her scalp. Thank god for the mud in the street. Dirt wet from the failed efforts to douse the fiery buildings with water provided a life-saving mixture

Standing in the street in her sleeping gown, her belongings burning inside, half her hair burned off…something happened which changed this traumatic tale into a story Anna would tell at Thanksgiving for years. A U.S. Army soldier said, "Miss, please take this coat…". Slipping off his heavy overcoat, this young sergeant wrapped it over her shoulders as she slid her hands through the arm holes and warmed herself into it. Her first smile in weeks lit her mud splattered face. The sergeant held her arm at the elbow and walked her down the chaos of Belmont Avenue toward the tent city the Army had set up next to the lake.

A couple days later, Hans arrived at the Union train station twenty blocks south where Canal Street and Adams cross. With his slowly improving English, he figured out that the Army had been sent to Chicago to restore order and provide temporary housing for the survivors. Hans literally walked every tent encampment the twenty blocks from Adams Street north to the Scandinavian neighborhood around Belmont Ave. There, where Belmont ends at the lake, he found the row of tents with Anna's name written on a tag strung to the flap door. During her week at this camp, she had accepted a "kit" the Army provided survivors. Managing to clean her face and arms, and with a new scarf and dress provided by the Army, she gratefully accepted an embrace and long hug from this grown up version of the Danish boy she only dimly remembered. She needed that hug. She yearned for it.

Anna and Hans were married in Elberta at the end of October, 1871. Hans brought a naturally pleasant, optimistic disposition to their union. Anna's warm shyness made for their sweet love and affection. They settled a farm on the road along the Betsey River less than a mile upstream from the harbor where Hans and his crew would dock and store their schooner for the winter. Seven children arrived in the world at that riverside farmhouse. One died in infancy. One of their sons married an Elliott. One of those sons became my grandfather, my mother's father. Such was the place we now call "home".

Anna made for herself a home. She provided nursing to the families of nearby Frankfort. She taught Sunday school, becoming a role model to my mother, great aunts and their daughters. When Anna arrived here in late 1871, this young Danish spinster only knew one thing. Home is what you build when you're reduced to nothing. Home is much more than a place or a house. It's creation itself.

#8 seems long. It's arduous. It's requires more than one well struck shot. It's a series of ups and downs. You just keep going. It's challenging. It's satisfying. It's a signature hole at the Downs. It's lofty and low. It's brings you up. You're heading home.

19

Thanksgiving

Warm light-hearted images of Thanksgivings past cushion my memories of family around hearth and home. These remembrances include the countless idiosyncratic foibles of siblings, parents, grandparents, aunts and uncle none more offbeat than those of my father's father, Donnell Avery.

Grandpa Don may have cornered the market for quirky food, beverage and bar gadgets. What would Thanksgiving be without a cordless electric turkey carving knife, or an ultra sleek glass froster (key to a properly chilled martini or old fashioned), and tin jello molds in the shape of an elaborate holiday flower wreath. Nobody could go deep on this most American holiday quite like the barbershop quartet singer from Bluffton, Ohio.

#9 at the Downs is an upper. It's compact and simple like Thanksgiving. The hole remains a short par three which plays up the hill back to the golf cottage. This little charmer of shingle and stone houses a Michigan white pine pro shop with a soup & sandwich counter and a wonderfully undersized and understated shoe room. The hole itself plays about 160 yards because of the elevated green. A bunker mines the right side of the putting surface protecting balls from bounding into the

fescue grass. While a short hole, the green can be daunting as it breaks and slants to the right front much more than it looks.

Thanksgiving traces its roots to celebrations of harvests and the end of the growing season. While Americans view it as uniquely American, the Canadians celebrate their own Thanksgiving in October. Japan, Germany, Caribbean Islands and Liberia all celebrate a similar autumn harvest festival. Early Thanksgiving feasts marked a time of goodwill and friendship with native Americans. Families often emulate this spirit with prayers and personal stories that honor the best that families promulgate as tradition and history. Bonds of family jell and deepen during this most familial holiday. You feel the warmth of ancestral figures, their stories, their ups and downs.

The ninth hole brings you back to where you started. Back at the beginning, you see where you came from and your roots. Families carry a culture down through the generations. Each culture extends itself through stories, the tales we tell through the family narrative. Just as the soil, ground and plants influence the wine that's made from grapes, our stories sweeten what it means to know and feel the love of family. Terroir comes from the French word which describes how the soil and plants alter the taste of grapes and the wine it creates. Terroir sounds much like terror. The terror of a great fire in Chicago, a cancer that returns, or a girl who steps on a nail only to die from the penicillin administered to conquer her infection. Just as these stories give a family its taste and sound, families carry them for the next generation. A gift to children not yet born. A gift that marks our love for one another.

Metaphors help sharpen the lens we apply to our stories. Helping to give texture and depth to what superficially can seem simple and plain. The metaphor of golf seems familiar to golfers. It can be new terrain for those not familiar with the ancient game. Given to me by a generous father, golf remains both a warm memory and living metaphor. As I address the ball and ease into a sandy stance, I hear those words, "quiet legs Kirk, quiet legs…". Letting go of a poorly struck shot, "think how good par will feel from there…". He and mom gave me so much. Mostly they gave me faith. A faith and optimism that forms a Thanksgiving, a time for gratitude and love. A love I gladly give to my children. A love that endures down through the ages to children not yet born.

20

VALE: White Christmas

How can the most popular Christmas song of all time be written by a Jewish composer? Maybe inherent in the great experiment of America lies the answer. A song about our most sacred holiday birth rooted itself in the emotion of Christmas, not the religion of Christmas. Irving Berlin working in Beverly Hills, California, longed for his family and children "up north" in snow covered New York State. The lost opening verse of this iconic song explains it all. Christmas may celebrate the birth of the man God; yet, it infuses us with the love and spirit of family.

The sun is shining, the grass is green,
The orange and palm trees sway.
There's never been such a day
in Beverly Hills, L.A.
But it's December the twenty fourth,
And I am longing to be up North—

Irving Berlin missed his family. He created an emotional appeal. Set in the opening battlefield scene of the movie "White Christmas", this song activates our memory grid.

Dreaming of family marks the lives of our military stationed in remote corners of the globe. They man the post, both men and women. They love our country. This hand cranked music box melody softly stirs the heart. "White Christmas" transcends race, ethnicity, religion and gender. Our most American of songs draws us back to the essence of love and family. You can picture the American GI setting his unshaven chin on the top of his field rifle listening to Bing Crosby's character Capt. Wallace crooning this connective melody. The GI dreams of Christmas past, probably his first Christmas.

My first Christmas memory finds me in my bedroom playing with the toy car and truck my parents placed inside my Yuletide stocking. My name "Kirk" knitted into the top border, it included these two little toy vehicles, along with a peppermint candy cane, miniature tinfoil holiday trees full of chocolate, and one large orange fruit. Hoping this stocking full of joy would pacify their five year old son long enough for them to sleep an extra hour on Christmas morning along with my own little baby brother. Glenn seemed like my own baby Jesus, except a little more colicky and an uneven sleeper.

When my parents finally awoke, they wandered out with baby Glenn to our living room decorated by our tinsel laden Christmas tree and a floor full of presents only to find no little Kirk. When they came to my closed bedroom door, they opened it. They saw me inside.

Playing contentedly with my little toy truck and car, I looked up at them. "Next year, can I have my presents under

the tree...?" My mom gulped...hard. Only then did she realize I thought these two toys were my complete Christmas. Only then did she realize that I was, in fact, quite content. I only hoped that next Christmas my presents could be under the tree like the other kids in the neighborhood. She knew right there, I was happy.

That very emotion would never leave my mom. She retells this story every year. It underscores for her the simple joy of Christmas. Gratitude and contentment marked her little son. She knew that she mothered me with just the right kind of affection and gave me peace. Mom could fill her own emotional Yuletide mug with the sweet satisfaction of Christian love. As a small family, we seem to strum the right cord at Christmas. With snow blanketing our Michigan home and lawn, we could truly enjoy "White Christmas".

Revisiting these memories both sweet and painful clears away the heaviness of the past. Into this absence what comes next? Into this absence, what presence take its place? Maybe that's what being present really means. Absence of cluttered unreleased memories leads to genuine presence. Sensory acuity becomes the new relaxed state. A state of mind that we value for itself, worthy of our effort to let go of the past.

As we close our eyes for the final time, an open hearted life lived present to others creases our face into a smile. A final wry smile that lets us leave this world at peace.

Vale can be used as a form of farewell or final salutation. Vale takes its Latin root from "to be worthy". Vale to you and those whose lives you touch. May they be worthy of your love and life.

PART III

ADVERSITY AS A GIFT

21

One More Motherless Kid

After young Donnell's mother died in 1911, the family placed him as a laborer at the neighboring Schmidt farm near Bluffton, Ohio. Farmer Schmidt made himself look generous to neighbors and fellow churchgoers by taking in the third oldest of the five brothers. However, in the evenings—after consuming a few pints—Schmidt thought it okay to use a motherless twelve year-old boy as a punching bag for his drunken pleasure. Let's just say that Don learned early how to avoid a punch. This skill came in handy later, when Donnell was an eighteen-year-old army corporal.

Not content to demonstrate an industrious spirit by running away from home at age thirteen, Don chose industry over glamour. Finding work in a Detroit fruit canning plant, he put down the Ohio plough and hay baler to make his way in big city America. Not averse to risk, he managed to make his way in this world at an early age, completely alone.

World War I dragged Europe into the slogging, mindless meat grinder of modern warfare. Young Don, however, saw the US Army and the war "over there" as a direct path to a dry bed and three squares a day. Don bought into Ty Cobb's observation, "I make my own luck." A young lieutenant named Dwight D. Eisenhower was his commanding officer. Watching this newly minted West Point graduate, Don learned up close

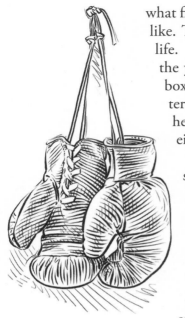

what firm, fair, and wise leadership looks like. Those lessons stayed with him for life. For his part, Eisenhower liked the young Midwestern farm boy who boxed his way to the Fort Dix welterweight finals, particularly when he realized that Don had just turned eighteen.

Literally hours after Don's ship, moored in New York Harbor, had been loaded with tanks and equipment bound for the battlefield, the war powers signed the Armistice ending the First World War. Young Don had avoided firing at the enemy. More importantly, he had avoided having the enemy fire at him. He had learned important lessons, however, and those lessons served him well after he returned to Detroit. Seeing firsthand the importance of steel to the production of tanks and military armor, he found work at Great Lakes Steel in their Ecorse, Michigan rolling mill. This time, Don's practice of "making his own luck" arrived in the form of Paul Carnahan. This young mill supervisor would become Don's lifelong friend—and eventually the president of Great Lakes Steel.

Young Don and Paul milled steel all week and spent their weekends hunting, fishing, and chasing the young ladies of Detroit. Meanwhile, Carnahan advanced through multiple promotions and began to circulate in the professional circles of the newly booming Motor City. Generously, he introduced Don to "Duke" Underhill, a successful young Detroit real estate owner and operator. Developing his sunny, engaging, and upbeat personality, Don managed with considerable effort to overcome his boyhood shyness and self doubt. He willed a way through his lack of confidence. Imagining himself successful, he viewed conquering his shyness as a prerequisite to good fortune.

In short order, Don became Underhill's top leasing and brokerage man. Eventually, he managed the business, and they became partners—Don was the good cop, Duke the bad—a partnership that survived the Crash of '29, the Great Depression, and the boom years of post—World War II Detroit.

On one of their many hunting trips out west, Don and Duke met their future wives during the long train ride to the Stanley Hotel in Estes Park, Colorado. Lily "Sally" and Marie Salathe were the daughters of Bay City, Michigan's town butcher, Frederick "Fritz" Salathe, and his wife, Anna. After high school, the two sisters moved to Detroit, where they worked at the Bank of the Commonwealth as executive secretaries. They maintained their love for horseback riding, and a week in Rocky Mountain National Park seemed like a trip of a lifetime. It was. They met Don and Duke on the train heading west. By the time they arrived back in Michigan, the two couples had fallen in love. With the invention of the telephone, these two sisters would call each other every day for the next forty-six years. Sisters marrying successful business partners and best friends, settling just a few blocks from one another—they thought they had hit the jackpot.

Don and Duke stood as best man in each other's weddings. Then they went back to keeping their small company growing during the Great Depression. Stumbling onto a need, they refocused their efforts on helping the banks appraise their foreclosures. They mastered the fine art of creating lasting relationships with the banks. They also grew skilled at appraisals—they could assess property from the running boards of their cars. Let's just say they were efficient.

The choice foreclosures could be bought before they hit the market. One man's misfortune can be another man's opportunity. Like golf, "every shot is good for somebody." Don and

Duke built up their small real estate company by buying foreclosure bound but well located properties. Industrious through the toughest of times, they turned the Great Depression into a seven-year buying opportunity.

Sentimental

How many husbands and fathers sit down with their sons and guide them through the process of handmaking Mother's Day and birthday cards? As a man who had lost his own mom at age twelve, Grandpa Don truly understood that love should be more than a feeling. It should be a behavior. His love could show up in the most unexpected ways. Handmaking holiday cards for his bride, Sally, seemed very natural.

When a seven-year-old boy wanders down the hallway of his grandparents' home in the middle of the night, he runs the risk of stumbling into something traumatic—or something innocent and sweet. Luckily for me, it was the latter. About once a month, my grandparents would take me for an overnight. It usually included going to their golf club, where I would learn to order a club sandwich and a Roy Rogers properly—"make that a double, and on the rocks." Don would then escort me around the dining room and introduce me to his friends. He would gently remind me to look everyone in the eye and shake everyone's hand. Combining his pride in his grandson with the opportunity to teach me how to carry myself around adults, Don demonstrated that love should indeed be a behavior, not just a feeling.

After working the room with Grandpa Don, we would head back for a family favorite—*The Jackie Gleason Show.* Gleason, Art Carney, and "Crazy Guggenheim" would make us laugh as I lounged on the living room floor in my pajamas. Eventually, after I fell asleep, Don would carry me to bed and put me under the covers. I wasn't supposed to wake up until morning.

One night, however, I wandered down the hall to my grandparents' bedroom. No one was there, so I continued down the other way to the "guest room." Though I failed to notice the room's décor, dusty pink with bold wallpaper, it was impossible to miss the painting of the beautiful, curvaceous, half clothed woman above the bed. Still, at seven years old, this room did not hold my interest. However, once I opened the door, my eyes grew large—real large.

Grandpa Don simply said, "It's perfectly natural, Kirk. Head back to bed, and Grandpa will tuck you in."

No shame, no big deal. Don could make things easy and smooth. Sentimental and loving, he loved his wife frequently. Equally important, she loved him. He loved his family without reservation. In his simple farm boy way, he taught us so much.

Humor

Between countless groaners and a steady stream of practical jokes, Don loved to laugh. He could laugh at himself. He could laugh at his friends. He could laugh at life. Looking back, I often wonder how he would have handled the modern world. My theory is that the Internet would put a real dent in his arsenal of practical jokes. Why entertain others when we can jump onto Facebook and entertain ourselves…by ourselves. By their very nature, practical jokes require group activity. At a minimum, one buddy needs another to make the joke come alive. These kinds of pranks became an art form for Grandpa Don.

A short list of some of Grandpa's comedic works of art:
- The chronic poacher at the Blaney Park hunting club, clad only in his pajamas, answered a knock at the front door of his cabin only to find two local "sheriffs" ready to arrest him for shooting a doe out of season. After the offender was cuffed,

in front of his wife, he was led to the backseat of Grandpa's oversized Lincoln. There, Grandpa and his old buddy, Duke, greeted him with a camera which captured the scared shitless look on his guilty face. He never poached again.

- Golfers at the Grosse Ile Golf and Country Club became accustomed to reaching into their golf bags for a new ball and finding the ball pouch filled with range balls. Why this struck Don as so funny, I'm not sure, but it happened often enough that pretty much everyone at Grosse Ile knew who did it. Let's just say that Don saw his share of range balls in his own oversized McGregor bag.

- What would possess a man to have the local Lincoln Mercury dealership install a car horn that made the sound of moose in the midst of their mating ritual in the woods? It's hard to describe startled pedestrians' reactions to the sound of a moose beginning connubial bliss. Is it funny? Is it harmless? Yes, on both counts. Does it make one wonder how strange things might have gotten on that farm in Ohio? Absolutely!

- As Grandpa faced the reality of cancer, his humor really shined. It's as if once he knew the cancer would win, he chose to use humor to overtake the pending sadness. One morning, when Duke was at his bedside, a nurse delivered the daily hospital breakfast—which included apple juice. Grandpa and Duke poured the apple juice into a clean bedpan, and when the nurse returned, they took out straws and began slurping it up. Initially, the nurse considered calling the psychiatric ward, but settled on reporting Don to the doctors as well on his way to "losing it." But Grandpa already knew by that point: he'd lost it.

Losing your mom at age twelve and being placed with another family leaves you stripped to the core. Maybe you realize at an early age that nothing—as in, no "thing"—makes you a complete person. It's your mind. It's your body. It's your spirit.

Donnell Avery worked hard for the rest of his life, conquering his bad spelling, reading biographical books and stories, and learning to read music. He worked on his mind every day. Boxing his way to the Fort Dix welterweight finals came easy. Learning to use his hands sparring with four brothers and a drunken farmer, Donnell used his body to fight, but he still knew when to make peace. Until the cancer, that strong body

never failed him. His spirit came out in his sunny sense of purpose. He loved his wife, Sally, and his sons, Donny and Ross, by serving their every legitimate need. He knew his example could live on well past the end of his physical life. It lived on through Donny and through his grandson, Kirk Donnell.

America knows the reality of motherless and fatherless children. It's not new. From the early years of disease in Colonial America, to the frontier wars in the West, to modern urban poverty, too many children have been dealt a bad hand of cards. Donnell Avery faced the same bleak future that many kids face. Luck helps. Hard work helps. Faith may be the tie-breaker. Don found plenty of all three—a lesson for all of us.

22

The Day We Were Shot

November 22, 1963, started with mom keeping me home from school for a visit to our pediatrician, Dr. Jones. Bucking up my confidence in advance of a measles vaccination shot, she fully succeeded. "Mom, I'm tough. They can give me the shot right here in my forehead." As I pointed with my little index finger to the front of my almost five year-old cranium.

Mom chuckled softly and said, "That won't be necessary. They'll probably give it to you in your arm or maybe your bottom."

"Okay, Mom, but I can do it.

"I'd begun in earnest, at an early age, to try to be tough like my dad, and Grandpa Don.

Mom kept me back from kindergarten that day to receive those pesky vaccinations all new school children should receive. She did a noble job of helping her eldest accept his shots like a big boy. She had no idea what we were about to walk into as mother and son.

"The President has been shot!" a nurse blurted out as she strode down the hallway between the patient rooms with penicillin spurting out the end of the syringe into her hands. Being nearly five years old, I looked up at my mom to see her face tense with confusion, then watched as the color drained out of it. We sat in our patient room while other children and their moms and I listened as voices rose from quiet murmurs to agitated expressions of horror and concern. Confusion of a young boy waiting for his shot on the same day our beloved President was shot through the front of his head.

The next stop of the day was the children's shoe store. My one year old brother Glenn had begun to walk. He needed new shoes. There, on an old black and white Zenith, Walter Cronkite surrendered the final word.

"The President died at one o'clock Central Standard Time. The official word has come—some thirty-eight minutes ago." Behind his large, dark-framed glasses, Cronkite tried to swallow his tears. That afternoon and the week of nonstop television coverage seared my memory. Like many young children in 1963, I felt really, really sorry for Caroline Kennedy. How could you not?

After the tragedy of the Twin Towers on September 11, 2001, trauma specialists began to describe how mediafed televised images themselves can lead to a form of PTSD. Children who try to understand these fragments of horror face the added difficulty of processing their parents' reaction to these same charged memories. Moms and dads made choices during those days after November 22nd and September 11th— choices about whether to allow children repeated exposure to Caroline starring at, and John-John saluting their father's casket; the riderless horse in a long, mournful cortège, Lyndon B. Johnson staging his constitutionally irrelevant oath of office swearing-in ceremony. Mom freely offers regret at sitting with me, glued to the TV for three days, and obsessing about the events stemming from the Dallas ambush.

But what about my dad? Here, this story takes a bizarre turn. Donny spent that weekend of November 22nd hunting for deer with Grandpa Don, the local high school golf coach, and the high school principal. Happily ensconced in their barely habitable deer cabin in remote Alcona County, Michigan,

Donny got his twelve point buck without interference from radio or television. As they drove south, back to Downriver Detroit on Sunday, November 24, 1963, they picked up the news coverage just north of Saginaw. They stared at the car radio in disbelief. For the next 100 miles, they caught up to what the country, mom, and I spent the previous three days processing. They heard through the radio what I had watched: the solemn caisson, John-John's salute, and live coverage of Jack Rubinstein thrusting that revolver into the stomach of Lee Harvey Oswald.

Donny dropped off grandpa and headed home. Strapped to the trunk of his '63 Thunderbird was the majestic buck dropped by a bullet right through the rib cage and furnace. Dad strode triumphantly through the front door in his red plaid hunting jacket and weekend of stubble. He did not get his customary flying tackle hug. Instead, I stood back in the living room at a distance.

"When I grow up, I'm going to be a good man like President Kennedy. Not a bad man what shoot things," I stated solemnly.

Dad glumly returned outside to his car as I followed him. Standing at the back of his T-bird, I began to pet in broad, slow, gentle strokes that magnificent stag.

My mother had a way of simplifying things. Giving her eyes the full side roll, she said plainly, "Donny, get that godforsaken deer out of here."

"Yes dear."

Donny drove to the local meat locker with his buck and dried blood covering the trunk of his car. One more memory file for review later in life. Maybe my fondness for John F. Kennedy "JFK," as he is often called comes from a deep place. The subsequent shooting of President Reagan once again brought me back to that deep place.

Fifty-two years later, a pediatrician's office once again held my attention. A simple sign hanging on the wall in the office of our grandson's doctor offered a thought provoking thought:

A CHILD WHO GROWS UP WITHOUT ENVY WILL NOT KNOW CONTEMPT.

Whatever my political leanings, the events of my child-hood cast me in a certain mold. My grandfather, Donnell Avery, served under Dwight D. "Ike" Eisenhower preparing for World War I, and again as a local Republican Party chair in 1952. Grandma Sally hung pencil drawings of Franklin Delano Roosevelt and JFK in the little sunroom she used for pinochle and bridge.

In summer 1980, when I arrived at her co-op to pour and mix her Crown Royal Manhattan and light her one daily Benson & Hedges menthol ultra thin 120 cigarette, she leaned over and whispered in my ear, "Don't tell your father, but I'm voting for Regan." I feigned alacrity and shock.

"Grandma! Whatever has come over you?"

She retorted, "That Carter is just a wuss."

Given my grandmother's pugnacity, you might wonder why listening to the virulent polemics of 2016 so offends me. In a nation marked by 250 years of growing freedom and lib-erty to individuals born to poverty and little property, our re-cent crop of political candidates spew vitriol and venom rath-er than sow the seeds of compromise, common ground, and progress. We've arrived at the time that Americans realize that government has become the tool for growing not narrowing the gap between rich and poor.

I guess I find myself thinking of that simple sign in that doctor's office. Where does the contemptuous rhetoric of 2016 originate? What happened in the lives of this current crop of candidates that leaves their speeches dripping with condescen-sion and arrogance for their self-imagined enemies and sup-porters? If contempt derives from envy, what spawned their envy? Was it lack of wealth? Lack of status? Lack of respect from others, their family, their parents, themselves?

With the recent passing of Nancy Reagan, the media seems to remember fondly both Presidents Kennedy and Reagan. Perhaps they're sentimental for a more civil tone of partisan politics. These archetypal Democratic and Republican presidents seem to act as bookends for the late twentieth century. One was born to great wealth; the other to rootless poverty. One was slighted as the grandson of an Irish bootlegger; the other as the son of the town drunk. One was raised in the rarified climes of Brookline, St. James Court, and Cambridge; the other in rural Tampico, Dixon, Des Moines, and Hollywood.

Why do these two disparate historical figures seem so bound together? How do men from such divergent backgrounds exhibit personalities devoid of the animus and venom of so many of their political brethren? Maybe we should consider a simple explanation: the strength of their mothers.

As rambunctious and reckless as the Kennedys could be, they all agreed that the matriarch, Rose Kennedy, represented the spiritual rock at the center of the Kennedy clan. Countess Rose Elizabeth Fitzgerald Kennedy typified the "lace curtain" Irish of upper-crust Boston. Unwavering in her loyalty to her risk-loving and unfaithful husband, Rose demonstrated a perseverance that wedded her children ever more tightly to her. Right up through her 104th birthday, her son Edward Kennedy fawned over her, extolling her for her steadfast character and fortitude. Considering that she survived five of her children, she exhibited a rectitude rare in public life.

Her strength in the face of the assassination of her son Jack defines dignity, class, and resilience to generations of Americans. Spending weeks walking the beach at her Hyannis, Massachusetts compound, she pleaded with God for an explanation.

"Why Jack? Why? It's simply not fair! So young. Healthy for the first time. Why?"

Privately mourning, Rose Kennedy remained ever stoic in public as the dignified matriarch. Her lofty spirit infused her son JFK.

"Mothers all want their sons to grow up to be president, but they don't want them to become politicians in the process."

These words, spoken by President John F. Kennedy, show that he keenly understood the purifying effects of his mother's guidance. Even his youngest brother, Edward, saw Rose in this sunny light:

> Mother was . . . our Pied Piper into the world of ideas. She led us on educational outings to museums and to concerts, to Concord and Bunker Hill and the Old North Church, rattling out improvised math challenges to us along the way . . . She was moderator of our topical dinner table conversation, the topics—geography one night, the front page headlines the next—announced in advance on cards that she wrote out and pinned to a billboard near the dining room.[1]

A daily observer of Mass, Rose loved her nine children with index cards and an occasional whack with a coat hanger. Banned to a dark closet, more than once a Kennedy kid realized that a sibling stood with them in the darkness. It wasn't the politically correct parenting of today's America, but these kids knew she cared—cared deeply—every damn day.

In daughter Eunice's words, "As we got older, [our father] made it possible for us to do things, but I think that the

---

[1] Barbara Perry. (2013) *Rose Kennedy: The Life and Times of a Political Matriarch* (New Your: W.W. Norton), 71.

[2] Perry, *Rose Kennedy,* 74.

terrific drive and everything, to me, came much more from my mother, than my father." [2]

Diminutive Rose Fitzgerald Kennedy demonstrated tough love. The Kennedys enjoyed an affectionate upbringing filled with privilege, but not a soft childhood—not soft in the least.

For young Ronald Reagan, on the surface, childhood couldn't have been more different. He would quip that living in an apartment above the town bank as an infant was the family's only association with a solid financial institution. These superficial differences in wealth and status, however, hid very profound similarities. Devout and spiritual enough to swear his presidential oath of office on his mother's bible, Reagan referred frequently to the impact of her strong Christian faith.

"I know she planted that faith very deeply in me."
—Placard, Reagan Family Museum
Dixon, Illinois

When visiting the family home museum in Dixon, Illinois, you're immediately struck by the emphasis on Nelle Wilson Reagan and her influence on the future president. Interestingly, his choice of college extended from his mother and her church, the Disciples of Christ. Reagan rose above truculence and blaming others. He lived a life of optimism forged through the exacting faith and influence of his mother.

From the Reagan Museum in Dixon, we learn that Nelle Reagan read scripture to prisoners in the town jail and would allow them to sleep in the Reagan guest room on their first night of freedom. Nelle extended her reputation as one of Dixon's best "readers" when she performed in the play *Ship of Faith*. It's hard to imagine that her public performances wouldn't someday influence her son as an actor, orator, and leader. Her example guided young Ron Reagan as he graduated from Eureka College, began a career as a radio sports broadcaster, and eventually served multiple terms as president of the Screen Actors Guild.

It seems unlikely that envy would bury itself in a soul filled with such a casual grin, and a deep and abiding humility. Even when delivering his famous speech at the Berlin Wall, Reagan exhorted Soviet leader Mikhail Gorbachev without contempt or condescension: "Mr. Gorbachev, tear down this wall."

Two presidents sharing the most important of influences: maternal acceptance, love, and discipline. Rose Kennedy and Nelle Reagan represent two mothers who understood the broadest scope of what endures in life, and the importance of imparting that to the spiritually healthy lives for which they were responsible.

The American people remain practical. How else can you explain our common affection for both President Kennedy and President Reagan? Setting aside ideology, we admire their willingness to roll up their sleeves and talk it through with their political adversaries. Knowing their fellow man to be human and flawed but still worthy of respectful discourse, they worked through the issues of the day. They made progress without resorting to condescension and contempt.

Let's tackle the essence of that sign hanging in the pediatrician's office. Without envy, children will not know contempt. Envy needs two people—or more—to become activated. Children compare themselves with others: siblings, cousins, classmates, or public figures in the popular media. Children unsure of their acceptance by others—particularly their parents—seek that acceptance elsewhere. Their lives become very self-centered; they obsess about themselves by constantly comparing themselves with others.

Envy seems to swim out of a river of narcissism. Just as Narcissus was obsessed with his own "image" in the river, some children become preoccupied with their own "self-image". This preoccupation obviates our connection to others. When we consider friends, family, or political figures, we often recognize narcissism in those who cannot enjoy and genuinely celebrate the success and happiness of others. The pained look of the narcissist when the spotlight shines elsewhere betrays that underlying weakness.

Listening to and *really hearing* our envy allows us to begin facing our doubts and fears, to come to grips with our weaknesses, and to start down a path of self-awareness that leads to confidence and a mindset without contempt. Leaving envy behind challenges us. The "clearing process" described earlier is a good starting point. Once we see the irrationality in ourselves, it becomes much more obvious when we observe it in others. We stop obsessing about what others think about us—what they possess, symbolize, or represent. We begin to understand and accept our own humanity and leave the envy and contempt behind, where it belongs. When we shine a light filled with humor, acceptance and warmth on our own flaws and foibles, we begin to radiate that charm we associate with those we respect, including beloved leaders and presidents. It all starts within.

23

Painted Helmet

Donny looked down at my green football helmet with the white tape down the middle and said to my mother quite plainly:

"Maggie, I put you in charge of raising these boys. What the hell kind of football helmet is that?"

"Don, he bought it with his own money at Montgomery Wards and right now State is, in fact, better...way better".

Dad grunted, "I'll handle things from here..."

Such was the turn of events that took me to my first college football game in Ann Arbor. Dad considered this first pigskin pilgrimage merely a midcourse adjustment in my unending passion for all things related to football.

Michigan State University did in the mid 1960's basically own the University of Michigan in football. Duffy Daugherty recruited immensely talented African-American athletes from the segregated south like George Aaron "Bubba" Smith and George "Mickey" Webster. He brought them to East Lansing. The student section would chant "Kill Bubba Kill!". These tall mobile behemoths would then terrorize opponents, and Big Ten schools either started to recruit these high caliber black athletes or they would pay a steep price for their prejudice. Competition once again proved that racial discrimination can be costly.

Donny chose the 1966 Michigan home game against Purdue as session one in the indoctrination of his eldest son as a Wolverine. That October day, we watched a spirited Michigan team play in front of a crowd of 79,000. Facing a top ten ranked Purdue team led by Bob Greise, Michigan lost 22-21. Still, Jack Clancy made stylish catches from Dick Vidmer along the sideline. Vidmer found Jim Detwiler, the "Toledo Tank" for another touchdown. Detwiler ran in a score. It was a close loss, but Donny prevailed. I was hooked.

ADDITIONAL STATISTICS

Official Attendance 79,642
Weather Conditions DRY FIELD CLEAR COOL

Score by Quarters:	1st	2nd	3rd	4th	Total
MICH	0	14	7	0	21
PURDUE	7	7	2	6	22

PRINCIPAL INDIVIDUAL PLAYS

List **all** scoring plays; also non-scoring plays (including punts) gaining 50 yards or more, and all **missed field goal attempts.**

Under "type of play" indicate rush, pass, int. runback, punt runback, kickoff runback, punt or field goal. List tries-for-points as P.A.T. kick, P.A.T. rush or P.A.T. pass.

On pass play, give passer first, then receiver, and combined yardage of pass and run. Measure runbacks from goal line, if started in end zone. Measure field goal attempts from point of kick. All other plays are measured from line of scrimmage.

Type of Play	Player or Players	Team	Yards	Scored?
PASS -	GRIESE to HURST	P	6	6
PAT K	GRIESE	P	0	1
PASS	Vidmer to Detweiler	M	35	6
PAT K	Sygar	M	0	1
RUSH	KEYES	P	11	6
PAT K	GRIESE	P	0	1
PASS	Vidmer to WARD	M	11	6
PAT K	Sygar	M	0	1
RUSH	Detweiler	M	1	6
PAT K	Sygar	M	0	1
SAFETY	TACKLED in ENDZONE	P	0	2
Blocked Punt	TEAM	P	0	6
PAT R	GRIESE	P	0	0
FGA	25 yd Sygar NG	M	0	0
Punts	Kemp	M	50	-
Punts	GRIESE	P	56	-
Punts	GRIESE	P	50	-

Returning home, I solemnly removed the white tape from my green helmet. Taking my Testors model spray paint, I dutifully painted my helmet dark blue and proceeded to try to paint maize yellow wings and three stripes in concert with my new found love, the University of Michigan Wolverines. They may have been the ugliest maize wings in the history of football art, but they were my wings. I was a convert.

Later, I learned two things. Dad wanted someone to share his love for the University. Sing "The Victors" with him during car rides. Listen to broadcasts on the radio while we fished the Betsey or Platte rivers. The other thing I learned didn't relate to football. He used U of M as a prod for doing better in school. He didn't need to say much when a mediocre report card arrived.

"You'll look just fine in green and white…" was about as harsh as dad could get.

He knew down under the banter and bluster that a perfectly respectable education could be earned in East Lansing.

Still, he used his Michigan degree as a prod. Quite simply, U of M was our family's school. Beginning with my maternal grandmother in 1926 and right on through Donny's grandchildren, our family often spends an early Saturday in May inside that same football stadium for another college Commencement. It started for me that October Saturday against Purdue. I loved that ugly hand painted helmet. It's part of who I am.

24

Sandcastles

"Would you stop throwing that damn wet ball against my clean wall!" Art rasped in a voice marinated by 50 years of Bulleit Rye and Kent Menthols. I smiled at him and waved, "How ya doing Mr. Childress?" As Mom later told me, Art found it hard to stay cranky at me. I was one of those kids who just never thought it was about me.

'Cause . . . it wasn't.

Afternoon showers soak Grand Bahama Island most every day around 3 p.m. during the summer. In the spring of 1968, Donny and Maggie retreated from the coming storm in Detroit and, with my brother and me, moved into a 12-story apartment building on the beach at Lucaya. At nine years old and being a bit too young for the casinos and beach bars, I settled on a future as a major league baseball shortstop. Knowing that the Tiger shortstop, Ray Oyler, couldn't buy a hit in a brothel, I figured my future was secure. My preparation began that summer. Art played the role of historian.

Hitting a baseball always seemed easier than fielding a baseball. So my tennis ball and I became fast friends. I would dutifully throw it against the cinder block stucco wall that surrounded the swimming pool filtration equipment on the parking lot side of the building. No problem. Every afternoon for hours I would emulate the sharp angle of an infield hit, scoop

it up, and throw it over to Tiger first baseman, Norm Cash, for the putout, 6 – 3 for you fans scoring at home. The beauty of this little game of mine was simple; I rarely made an error.

Not so at our new school, St. Paul's Methodist. "Humbled" became a verb I learned very well that spring. Mom was a school teacher and took a job teaching middle school English at an American Catholic School on the island. Her school, Mary Star of the Sea, didn't really fit the Ayn Rand devotee of the late 1960s and yet they hired her immediately upon seeing her diploma in philosophy and classics from the University of Michigan. Sister Mary Alice had no clue that she had just hired her first radical libertarian subversive. Things were about to get very interesting for the Italian nun from South Philly.

Being thoughtful, Mom sent my brother Glenn and me to the British parochial school on the other side of town. She knew full well how hard it could be for kids to have a mom teaching in the same school. Her mom had done exactly that to young Maggie Bjornson. Schooled in the same building where her mom taught may have been the first of multiple PTSD episodes she endured as a young schoolgirl. Grandma was a tough cookie; tougher than hardened molasses. Little Maggie was on the receiving end of that setup from kindergarten right up to the ninth grade. She escaped to high school fully hardened to the ways of the world in more ways than one.

St. Paul's Methodist School came as quite a shock to a kid who spent all nine years of his life being told he was utterly brilliant. Methodist, as in the one and only method of schooling the young children of the British Empire, included morning chapel, merit cards and badges, the Queen's English spoken precisely, and your multiplication tables memorized to 12 unless you wanted to be struck by a tennis ball in the chest if you became inattentive during math class. A morning Bible reading followed by a thorough indoctrination in the superiority of Britain as a colonial superpower would, on occasion, strike this young Detroiter as fairly preposterous. For instance, being told that the Kingdom stood alone during the Battle of Britain while the Americans sat on their arses didn't really go over very well for a family born and raised in the Arsenal of Democracy. As Dad liked to point out, if it weren't for Henry Ford and Rosie the Riveter, these dear sweet folks would be seiging "Heil Hitler" between visits to their departed family at the nearby concentration camp. A battle of patriots to say the least—patriots who all happened to settle on Grand Bahama Island during the miniboom of the late 1960s.

In 1955, the British Parliament had passed the Hawksbill Creek Act. The Act established a port authority which governed the large, natural harbor bisecting the western half of the island. It mandated that there would be few taxes of any kind for 99 years. However, levying a 20 percent duty on all goods (except peas and rice) that hit the docks helped fund the roads, sewers, and utilities that provided the kickstart that the island economy needed. With only a hundred residents in 1955, the island population swelled to over 30,000 by the time our family arrived in 1968. The government funded a series of elementary schools that dotted the small villages of the island. More importantly, the three parochial schools fully integrated themselves racially and religiously from day one. An experiment in free enterprise which included immigrants from every corner of the world, and a genuine mix of schools and churches.

This island represented a refuge for my increasingly cynical parents. The assassination of President Kennedy in November of 1963 traumatized the nation. My parents seem to take it even harder. Dad knew the military from the perspective of a JAG officer in the Army. He became aware of some nasty secrets—stuff they saw in the course of their work. The idea that a social misfit like Lee Harvey Oswald had pulled off the assassination by himself struck this former prosecutor as patently absurd. To both Donny and Maggie, watching the aftermath of LBJ cloaking himself in civil rights and twisting the movement into an extensive government transfer program seemed beyond grotesque. Watching their native Detroit become the laboratory hothouse for a running series of government planning efforts was the last straw. Quite simply, they gave up on America. At least the America that LBJ led into Vietnam and his domestic government planning utopia. By late 1967, our family was fully committed to a pullout—a pullout from Detroit and America.

This is that story.

Methodry

"Abigail Johnstone"—the name, not the person—appeared at the top left corner of the chalkboard in our classroom. Across the top of the board, Mr. White listed the subjects we'd learned during the 1967-68 school year: arithmetic, reading, writing, etc. Below each subject was a number. The score for each student in that subject was there, out in the open for everyone to see. For the 24 kids in the class, 24 scores in arithmetic, reading and writing. In the aggregate, Abigail was first. I was 21st—not exactly an utterly brilliant performance for the future Tiger shortstop. We arrived in March and I managed, in three short months, to land myself in the cellar, more like a Washington Senator than a Detroit Tiger.

The best part? There was no pattern to the ranking of students. You couldn't group them by race or religion or nationality. There were probably more girls at the top of the list, but there were exceptions randomly distributed everywhere. This was a true meritocracy. By the way, Abigail Johnstone not only sounded Bahamian; she looked it. Lean and pretty with big, bushy pigtails, you could imagine generations of Abigails cleaning their husbands' catch of the day, steaming up the peas and rice, baking the Johnnycake and making more Johnstones and Farquarsons and Pinders. Except this one would go to college someday.

St. Paul's Methodist School made itself such that the Queen would be proud. Kind of like Americans in the south think of themselves as more patriotic than the average American (horseshit). The Methodists in England came from their "west." Being so far from London, they seem to work a little harder at being British.

Methodists in many ways are like Baptists in America, except they can read. Stern in temperament, knowing how to have fun was not something they seem to master or cared to master. It probably didn't occur to them. They were too busy perfecting themselves, their children and their workdays. Margaret Thatcher was a Methodist. That explains a lot. She was a Methodist whose father owned a grocery store. Geez, that would have been exciting. No wonder she would lecture her Cabinet on the price of a gallon of milk. Upper crust Tories must have loved that speech. Hell, those guys probably never saw a kitchen, much less a grocery store. It's no wonder she finally succumbed to a "no confidence" vote. Those Tories had absolutely zero confidence in their ability to endure so much fun and laughter. Let's just say that these Methodists at

St. Paul's came by their stern, exacting personalities naturally —naturally drilled up their backsides one shilling at a time.

I used to wonder how they reproduced. Did they schedule time for it during the day? Did they grade it? Did they practice? Could you earn a merit badge? Spontaneous romance and "grinding," as the Bahamians like to call it, seemed a far off homework assignment for these Methodist teachers at St. Paul's. It wasn't enough that you completed your work assignment accurately and punctually and in ink. Cursive writing which was blotted or crossed out earned a terse admonition of "points deducted, young man!" In order to earn the prized merit card, everything must be nothing less than perfect. Five cards in a week earned you a merit badge.

The school divided its student body into four "houses" across all "forms" (grades to us Americans). As a nine year old, I entered the second form in March, having just left third grade in America. The four houses derived their names from the most famous of the British explorers: Schackleton (blue), Mallory (green), Hillary (red), and my house, Hudson (yellow). The merit points led to a yellow badge for yours truly, although not as often as I thought I deserved. Every term, the points for each house were tallied and added to the other house's totals in athletics and drama. Everything, and I mean EVERYTHING, counted for something. Either it was added to your tally or, God forbid, it could be deducted from your total.

Morning chapel provided an excellent opportunity for me to have points deducted. It's not that I rejected the Christian faith completely. It just seemed to interfere with my opportunities to debate the great issues of the day with my buddies. Issues like the relative value of marbles—milkies vs. cat eyes; the superiority of American football over rugby and soccer; who was prettier: Kim Goodwin or Roselyn Abrahams. These were profound subjects worthy of extensive debate. The Methodists disagreed.

As point totals went, let's just say two points forward and one point back seemed to be my natural rhythm. Did I learn? You betcha. When your mother is a school teacher, this whole education thing you do as a kid is kinda the family business. You can't be a total putz. So, I began to learn my cursive letters a bit more elegantly. I scored high in reading, owing mostly to the long articles in my Dad's copies of Penthouse and the Miami Herald sports section. Mostly, it was the multiplication and division of fractions that haunted me. I didn't plan to own a grocery like Mr. Roberts (the Iron Maiden's father). Why did I need to know how to price milk in pints, quarts and gallons? But learn I did. Repeating this stuff for another year would have been far worse. The more I thought about my name appearing 21st on that chalkboard, the more determined I became. Hell, let's admit it—by the time we moved back three and a half years later, I was fourth in the form. The methodry worked.

Tiger Art

Art Childress hailed from the thriving metropolis of Owosso, Michigan, population 14,779 and dwindling by the hour.

As for many taxpayers, America was losing its charm and nowhere more so than in the Wolverine State. Art finally waved the white flag of surrender in 1966 and landed a job as the property manager for the Rivera Towers apartment building on the south shore of Grand Bahama Island. Our paths crossed the first time he identified the culprit throwing a wet tennis ball against his pristine stucco wall.

You cannot see the irrationality of others until you see it in yourself. Occasionally, Art would caution me to do as my mom would say, "Your mom is not being critical, she loves you. That's how moms make sure you do right. . . " Thinking back to that "clean wall", maybe Art endured more than his fair share of criticism from his mom. I wonder 'cause he sure seemed committed to keeping that wall clean.

As a young boy, Mr. Childress seemed cranky and more than a bit didactic. Still, instead of berating me for making a mess of his wall, he decided to distract me with an oral history of baseball. In his manager's apartment, his shiny aluminum Philco pulled in the Atlantic Braves broadcasts from West Palm Beach, Florida—their spring training home. With their announcer, Dizzy Dean providing the sound track, Art colorized baseball as few would hear it. Granted, this longtime Tiger brought a certain homespun bias. Best hitter of all time? Ty Cobb, of course. Best second baseman? Charlie Gehringer with his .320 average, 2800 hits and League MVP in 1935. Best catcher? Mickey Cochrane. Best slugger who served his country honorably? Hammerin' Hank Greenberg. Well, you get the idea.

Art saw in me what a priest sees in a soul that might be saved. For me, baseball still hung in the balance with football, and Art simply could not stomach the idea that a young baseball soul might be lost. With the help of the Tigers playing some very, very good baseball in the summer of 1968, Art had his convert. The Braves moved to Atlanta only two years earlier—(part of my education was learning how they migrated from Boston to Milwaukee to Atlanta). Dizzy Dean had played for the St. Louis Cardinals.

As the Cards marched to the National League pennant that season on the back of Bob Gibson, old Art couldn't resist pointing out that Dizzy Dean was the best pitcher but only in the NATIONAL LEAGUE during his career. The Tigers (of course) offered the best pitcher in all of baseball during the World War II era. Harold "Prince Hal" Newhouser, who won pitching's Triple Crown in 1945, led the Tigers as they beat the Chicago Cubs for the World Series.

Each day passed and soon school started again in the Bahamas in September. Art kept me off that stucco wall with his personal narrative on the history of the American pastime. Learning American baseball in the Bahamas was kind of surreal when you think about it—but he did manage to keep his wall clean. Like a pitcher and an outfielder at Fenway, we worked that "wall" together. Eventually, he'd throw those hard infield grounders to me himself. The old coot actually started to like me. In the end, when the Tigers clinched the pennant, I think he considered me his good luck charm. This husky little Tigers fan in-the-making actually could make him laugh as I personally narrated my own stylish fielding and throwing. And Art had forgotten how to laugh.

The Tigers spotted the Cards a 3-1 lead in the '68 World Series; then the two Mickeys took over. The occasionally sober Tiger manager, Mayo Smith, made the first of a couple of brilliant moves. Beefing up the batting order meant moving Mickey Stanley from the centerfield to shortstop. Presto, the Tiger infield batting average instantly made it above the Fahrenheit boiling point.

Next, old Mayo pressed Mickey Lolich into pitching the seventh game. This meant Lolich could do something historic. Not only would the Tigers rally from down 3-1, Lolich would pitch and win three complete games in one World Series. Old Mr. Childress couldn't believe how good it all was. Late in Art's life, living with a cancer I only learned about later, his beloved Tigers won the World Series. Plus, he saved one more soul from Yankeedom. Tiger Art 1—Yankees 0.

Less is More

Within ten years of the passage of the Hawksbill Creek Act, the northernmost island in the Bahamian archipelago saw its population mushroom from a mere 100 to over 30,000 sun-kissed inhabitants. How? In a world where we debate endlessly how to alleviate poverty and create jobs, how did this little outpost do it?

The natural assumption would be that it was all tourism. This was logical given the sunny temperate weather, cool night breezes and squeaky, white sand beaches. Yet, throughout the '60s, as Grand Bahama grew and changed, tourism never reached 50% of the island's domestic economic output.

British Petroleum built a large oil transport center, which employed a steady 500-800 workers. Syntex built a pharmaceutical plant which added another 80-100 jobs to the island. A large cement plant, which predated the Hawksbill Act, continued to employ a steady crew of 50-60. The only other significant employer was NASA, which built the Gold Hill Tracking Station for the Cape Canaveral rocket launches. No single employer or industry explains what happened on this 100-mile long stretch of coral and southern pine.

During this time, Daniel K. Ludwig of Denmark reigned as one of the world's great shipping magnates. He lived part-time on the island, mostly checking on his shipping businesses in the Caribbean basin. Desi Arnaz and Lucille Ball retreated to the island frequently in search of privacy and seclusion, yet the wealthy really didn't discover Freeport/Lucaya in droves. If an economy ever came to be defined by a broad, wide and deep middle class, it was Grand Bahama Island of 1963-71. Maybe the greatest irony for our family arose in comparing it to Detroit during this same time period.

Our old home town had grown to be America's fourth largest city in 1950 with a middle class powerhouse the world could only envy. Detroit was marked by the highest median household income and home ownership of any major city. What followed can only be described as a seemingly endless string of crony mayors from both political parties who allowed Detroit to become an experimental urban laboratory for government planners of all stripes and persuasions.

Urban Renewal obliterated sixty square blocks of stable residential and commercial property owned mostly by long time African-American families. Later known as Lafayette Park, it became another of Detroit's once mighty neighborhoods reduced to blight and abandonment. "Model Cities" concocted by LBJ's "War on Poverty" managed to move the poor into new parts of the city. Meanwhile, another half million Detroiters took the government's subsidies and simply left.

Many would say racism and corporate greed fueled the demise of Detroit. Of course, Detroiters struggle with the idea they carry more racial amicus curiae and avarice than the good people of Chicago or Boston or Pittsburgh. In Detroit, if there was an urban planning experiment that could qualify to receive funding, they tried it: a wide freeway through an established neighborhood, a city income tax, commuter tax, low income housing, public housing, the People Mover. If the government funded it, the crony mayors tried it. In short order, the city residents figured out they weren't welcome, because in fact, they weren't. As in life, sometimes when it comes to government, less is more.

Civil Disobedience

Rooted in the writings of Henry David Thoreau and then blooming into the flower of Mahatma Gandhi and eventually Dr. Martin Luther King, our world elevated itself mightily from their common moral high ground. Racial discrimination rightly thrust itself into the American consciousness during these same 1960s. Grand Bahama provided an illuminating and intriguing vantage point despite being a mere sixty miles off the Florida coast.

Slavery predates Jesus of Nazareth. The freedom he offered through the Kingdom of God transcended slavery as chattel. He offered freedom at a deeper level. Freedom from our own flawed humanity took liberation to a new, higher moral and spiritual plain. In every direction, people sought greater freedom and dignity. Breaking out of the shackles seemed all the rage in the 1960s. Everyone got into the act, even the students at St. Paul's Methodist.

What were we thinking? Bologna sandwiches on white bread with butter—and we didn't love them?

"Do you know how little we had during the Second World War?"

"Do you know we didn't even have sugar or fruit or orange juice?"

Geez, no, I didn't and, by the way, that was twenty-nine years ago and you really can't blame me. I'm eleven!

Only one option existed. I'm going to lead these fellow eleven-year olds to some decent food. We're going to town —to Burger King. Not my best planned act of civil disobedience. When virtually all of the eleven-year olds disappear from an elementary school, chances are high the teachers will notice. It just doesn't happen often enough to slip past them. So, waiting for us at the front of the line? You guessed it. A direct descendent of the first King of Scotland; our stern, inchoate but loving headmaster, Eric "The Red" Williams. Yep, there he was, all 6-foot-3-inches and 225 pounds (16 stone for you true Brits) smiling at his seventeen wayward Fourth Form eleven-year olds. Caning was reserved for yours truly. You need to plan a crime to feel the full arm of the law. I received it and managed not to cry or yelp. I actually felt sort proud; an odd reaction for the son of a school teacher.

I wondered if the real, genuine protestors felt the same way. The year before, it was Dr. King who was shot and then Robert Kennedy, the brother of the slain President. Our parents couldn't help but question the civil unrest broadcast on TV each night. These people must be partially right—some of this must be justified.

Race in America can appear as a two dimensional issue. America mixes race and slavery into a toxic brew that haunts us to this day. Elsewhere in the world, racial discrimination exists. It took America to bind slavery into racial discrimination. Not so in other countries. In the Bahamas, the pecking order works in a simpler way:

Bahamians look down on Jamaicans.

Jamaicans look down on American Blacks.

American Blacks down on Haitians.

Bermudians look down on everybody.

By 1970, Bahamians seemed intent on gaining independence, but it didn't involve race and it didn't involve civil disobedience. It was their country and they were free to do their will. That's exactly what they did. Foreigners were deported. The island economy came to a standstill. Non-Bahamians saw their work permits revoked. Capital fled. It was now their country—poorer, but free of foreigners. It wasn't race that drove the middle class away. It was much simpler. It was fear. It was a fear of foreigners.

It was all over. The middle class disappeared. In time, you were either a tourist or a Bahamian, or eventually a narco drug lord. Grand Bahama went the way of Detroit. Like a sandcastle, it just washed away. Such a shame—twice in one childhood.

Attracted to Risk

A twelve-story apartment building on the south beach of Grand Bahama sure seems like the wrong place for a nine-year old boy to play. And it was. Designed like many Bahamian apartment buildings, the front door to each unit opened to an exterior, outside hallway. Problem! Then, the elevator stack was wrapped on the outside with a staircase that candy-caned itself to the roof of the twelve-story building. Problem! Probably not the best choice for young families with young children.

For moms and dads who dreamed of living on a beach of beautiful, squeaky, white sugar sand, they found nirvana at Rivera Towers. Weekends included all these young families picnicking around the lawn that joined the open breezeway lobby to the beach itself. With seven units on each floor and families in the larger two and three bedroom units, there were lots of kids for play and mischief.

Why did that roof seem so interesting? As a nine-year old, I wondered if you could see Florida from there—(that would be a "no"). The locked door at the outside staircase really didn't slow us down. It did require climbing around the wooden door jam that Art Childress built to prevent residents from doing exactly what we did. That would be climbing up onto the railing and around the outside of that wooden door and door jam. Lucky for us that we didn't slip or lose hold and fall the twelve stories down to the grass landscaped entrance. That would have been a sight . . . splattered nine-year olds landing right outside the apartment leasing office. I do wonder if my extreme acrophobia might just stem from scaring the shit out of myself and then carrying and blocking that memory into a place that I can no longer access.

Sean Connery wrapped up the filming of *"Thunderball"* in 1965 with the help of the divers from UNEXSO about a mile down the beach from Rivera Towers. Few movies stimulated scuba diving like *"Thunderball."* Moviegoers watched Connery and Claudia Auger canoodling among the sea fans and coral and assumed they could do the same with a few lessons.

Dad and I took to scuba quickly and completely. Starting with the twelve to eighteen foot reefs and graduating to wrecks of sunken ships and grotto caves. Donny and I tried them all. Only when the depths exceeded 100 feet did Dad bow out and let his now eleven-year old son keep going. Guided diving trips from Grand Bahama and the UNEXSO club replaced Little League and Boy Scouts.

Below one hundred feet, double tanks allow you twenty to thirty minutes at depth to explore and then to fully decompress as you rise. Off Grand Bahama, beginning at eighty-five feet, the ocean floor begins to noticeably drop until at approximately one hundred and ten feet, it goes vertical. Going over that edge gives you the feeling of being suspended over the pitch dark ocean floor and provides a very genuine rush of adrenalin. That euphoria makes the dive worth the hassle of decompression. Dad disagreed. Also, we decided not to tell Mom about the sharks, that poor woman had enough to worry about.

Let's talk sales. The kid needed some walking around and scuba cash. Selling newspaper subscriptions door-to-door would be the slow, safe way to win a sales contest. The top ten subscription sellers won an autumn weekend in Miami to watch the Dolphins host the Cleveland Browns. I opted for

the accelerated sales strategy, writing all of my parents' and grandparents' friends in Detroit and suggesting they might want an off-island subscription (worth three times as much in sales contest credit). Let's just say I won this trip going away . . . and pissed off all the older newspaper boys. I did enjoy every last envious smirk. Photographed at the top of the stairs for the Air Bahamas flight to Miami, I needed to stand on my tippy toes to appear as tall as the other winners.

Memories of that weekend with the Dolphins at the old Orange Bowl seem dim. The Browns dumped the 'Phins 28-0. What I do remember was fellow newspaper man, Harry Palm, upchucking his eleven twelve-cent burgers from the White Castle hamburger joint onto the moving escalator at Jordan Marsh in the North Miami Beach Mall. Watching the poor janitor chase the befouled escalator step rising, rising, rising and then disappearing again and again is a memory I probably should block. Winning remains the best part. With winning, came confidence.

Perhaps, I developed too much confidence. I don't know how to sail. In fact, a rudimentary understanding of sailing escapes me. Therefore, the decision to sail our friends' sunfish to the west end of the island seemed highly suspect, particularly for an eleven-year old. Compounding matters, I chose the week of my parents' annual anniversary vacation for this poorly conceived sailing excursion. Not content to drive my parents a little cuckoo, I gave my grandparent babysitters full-on angina. When they couldn't see their grandson on the southern horizon, the shit was definitely going to hit the fan. And I knew it. How did I manage to reverse tack my way to a half mile off shore? I didn't know how to sail on a whole new level.

Let's just say Grandpa Don, with the wrath of Hades, greeted his favorite grandson upon swimming the sunfish (with the rope line in my mouth) back to the Rivera Towers beach. I guess my only fear was of my grandparents' reaction once I solved this self-created problem. Grandma Sally usually overlooked my transgressions, but not that night. What was the attraction to risk? Probably the completely irrational mindset that nothing bad would ever happen to me. As fate would have it, that changed later.

Back to Mom, our first subversive libertarian radical. While Dad chummed up the Bahamian officials in the process of strategically selling them his new condos, Mom would occasionally stand in the Winn Dixie parking lot changing Bahamian money into American dollars for the Haitians. Dad's protection from his Immigration and Customs buddies gave him little comfort when Mom was loudly challenged at one of their weekend cocktail parties. However, this didn't stop old Maggie. Her mission wasn't subverting the value of the Bahamian currency. No. Rather, she saw in these poor Haitians a proud people who simply wanted to send American dollars back to their families. "You risk taker Mom…carry on, Maggie!"

Dad had a knack for naming condos. Fairway Manor seemed a touch too baronial for what he actually built on the 16th hole of the Ruby golf course. Seriously, Dad? *Edelweiss Chalets?* Let's try that one more time.

He really hit his stride with the Edelweiss Chalets at the corner of Santa Maria and Nina Boulevards. This drew in the local government officials who never thought they would live in an neo Austrian condo project on the beach in the Bahamas —a regular marketing impresario, that old Donny.

If your two favorite stories are *"The Sound of Music"* and *"The Godfather,"* you are psychologically predisposed to name your landmark condo project Edelweiss Chalets and fill it with croupiers and mildly corrupt local officials. "Bless Our Homeland Forever." "Keep your friends close, keep your enemies closer." Such was the attraction to risk.

As I write these memoirs of childhood days in the Bahamas, a small, copper boating tub with a makeshift sail made landfall in front of The Delano Hotel on Miami Beach. Five bedraggled, sunburned Cubans and a frightened teenage girl, still dazed from their 36-hour journey, sat next to their makeshift craft. The bar maids from The Delano served them water and non-alcoholic mixers, while tourists with iPhones snapped pictures of the sailors' grinning mugs and their crazy little craft. It reminded me of the Haitian shipwrecks Dad and I explored with scuba gear in the Bahamas, mailboats with too many Haitians on board that made it close enough to the beach that these risk takers could swim or walk the rest of the way. In many ways, the world sees this every day.

In short order, American politicians will condemn these beneficiaries of our "Wet Feet—Dry Land" policy for Cubans seeking asylum in America. Some politicians will demonize them as illegal immigrants. Others will wait until they're multi-millionaires and vilify them for their financial success. I prefer to admire their attraction to risk and a country that rewards it. God Bless America and every damn risktaker who found their way here. We wouldn't be America without them. We're lucky.

25

Walking Life Lesson

Learning how to swing a golf club from dad at Crystal Downs did not mean I learned all the lessons of life offered up by that game at a such tender age. No, the most enduring and uplifting lessons came later with my father and his golf buddy "Slaw". Slaw was the nickname given to him at the local Bahamian golf club. Slaw became bigger than life for me as a young boy. Despite his small stature, he taught us a long list of lessons. Slaw lived as an immigrant. Overcoming painful and deep trauma, he personi-fied class and character. He owned a genuine smile. He offered honesty to a fault. These lessons walk with me to this day…

Slaw became a hero over Dunkirk in 1941. Born Zdizslaw Radomski near Kruszwica, Poland in 1915, he fled

as a young Air Force pilot with the German occupation in late
1939. Always one to protect those who protected him, his
escape story lacked much detail. Needless to say, this young
Flying Officer used his Polish Air Force plane to cross into
Romania. Making his way to Oran and Casablanca, he eventually booked passage to Liverpool, England. After fighter
training in Bristol and Scotland, he found his calling among
his countrymen.

Assigned to RAF Squadron 306 made up of Polish officers, it didn't take long for Slaw to shoot down four Me 109s
soon after earning his first Spitfire. These early successes over
Cherbourg earned him more and more assignments. He was
fighting for country and a great cause.

Fate found him on August 21st, 1941 over Dunkirk
when Flying Officer Capt. Radomski took a 20mm cannon
shell through his Spitfire into his upper left arm, just above
the elbow. Slaw described how the shell seem to melt the mus-
cle, skin and bone. The heat of the shell burned through the
nerves. Heat so intense, he could not feel it. He could only
recognize that it couldn't be stopped. The arm would never
return. It was gone as it fell limp inside his uniform.

Managing to fly back across the Channel he landed his
plane at Northolt. Near the seaport city of Deal in Kent, the
airplane ground crew couldn't quite grasp how this barely
conscious pilot with his severed left arm hanging inside his
uniform managed to fly and land this plane safely. He flew on
instinct. Through his daze, he imagined the sequence to land.
Sensing a landing can be almost the same as actually touching
down the wheels. He knew it cold.

A blood transfusion and amputation saved his life.
Continuing to serve despite no longer being able to fly, Slaw
became a navigation and flight controller. He used his bilingual
skills in support of the many Polish air squadrons stationed
in England during World War II. Eventually, reassigned back
to Northolt where he sustained his earlier injuries. He served
right up to the end of the war in 1945, even opening a night

club in London that became a favourite haunt of the exiled Poles still living in England.

Although he returned briefly to Poznan, a college town on the Warta River in western Poland, he could see that Poland as a free country was slipping away. Using his amputation as cover with the medical staff, he slipped out a hospital window. He'd managed to escape a prison the Communists used for Poles who could not make peace with the new puppet government. His cadre of subversives and his wife proved not to be so lucky. Then and there, he dropped martyrdom as a mask. He let go of the last remnant of feeling sorry for himself.

This time, there would be no return to Poland. Slaw became a bona fide immigrant upon gaining citizenship as a British subject. In fact, England welcomed this war hero as one of their own. Welcoming Slaw didn't, however, mean that they would tax him fairly; or the thousands of successful Brits who fled Britain's crushing tax rates of the 1960's. Like the Beatles, countless scientists, inventors, doctors and business owners, Slaw recognized that success in life pivoted from a person's ability to adapt and change. Change came intuitively to Slaw. One change did, however, catch him by surprise. His time in London led him to one new awakening—his stunningly striking and graceful second wife, Judy.

On Grand Bahama Island, in the late 1960's, it was hard to miss Slaw and Judy. Outshone by a lean, lithe and radiant wife, even a one arm war hero and golfer found it hard to be noticed. Silky smooth in her kindness, Judy won over anyone within earshot or with decent eyesight. She looked at you and you just melted into her incandescence. When she and Slaw would drive off in his azure blue Bentley convertible for a night on the town, they seemed larger than life. They transcended the typical labels and standard norms. Love fluttered and flew between them on every level.

An eleven year old boy grows up a little faster once he sees first hand a person whose beauty goes well past skin deep. Judy looked at Slaw as a man who climbed very far above his working class roots. Her gaze upon this taut muscular one arm war hero brought a smile and glow across her face. Love can sometimes be a hope—a hope in the promise or potential of a person or a spouse. This promise became real that first evening she heard the other Poles standing in their London pub describing one of their great countrymen and how he made their world a better place. Not just by shooting down German Messerschmitts, or winning medals of valor. Slaw made the world better by how he lived his life. Rejecting martyrdom, he let the world in on his secret. Those around Slaw could see themselves improved simply by knowing him. They were led by his example.

It all became obvious on a golf course. Few games require a counter intuitive mindset like golf. He held his left handed golf club with his right hand. We think we swing a golf club with our hands and wrists. Actually, we begin the swing of a golf club with our shoulders. Slaw had two of those. We need to keep our head still. Slaw mastered that early. Great golf swings remain compact. Slaw exuded compactness. Mostly, golf requires humility and managing expectations. In this realm, Slaw was unbeatable. Few people appreciated a simple day like Slaw. He understood more than most that he was lucky just to be alive. Add in his loving, radiant wife, his home high above a sandy Bahamian beach, and Slaw understood that a disappointing round of golf was one more day in paradise. By letting go of the outcome, the quality of the outcomes improved.

Eleven year old boys want to be normal, like the other kids. Here was a guy unlike everybody I ever knew, or would be likely to ever know. And, he was really good at it. The day my father introduced me to Slaw Radomski and I shook his very strong right hand, being different would start to seem okay. I could start to be me.

26

Fork in the Road. Take it

"**K**eep the doobie down…not so obvious", as Kip passed it back to Raleigh, he swept the joint low across the dashboard right past old Rennie. Getting Raleigh stoned far outweighed in importance sharing this Acapulco Gold equitably with his long time ski buddy. Raleigh loved Kip, and Kip loved Raleigh. So did most of the male graduates of Boulder High. 19th century shipbuilders would have enjoyed the process of carving Raleigh on the prow of a ship. "Rales" as friends knew her, sported a fine, lithe and ample chassis on her long, lean legs. Kip was not about to waste this last chance at an afternoon of lovemaking before returning to UVA for the fall semester.

As he turned the ignition to the family station wagon, Rales drew in a long, slow drag on this all but expired bone. Cemeteries made great spots for a quick smoke. The Hill Cemetery at Ninth and Pennsylvania offered the added benefit of stands of Colorado blue spruce for privacy and seclusion. Drop Rennie at Boulder High where his mom worked, and Rales could give Kip the going away present that would keep him coming back from Charlottesville at Thanksgiving and Christmas. She let her hair out of the band, and shook it out loose and long. Kip managed to sneak the car through the yellow light at Broadway and University. At that point, Rennie piped up. "Just drop me at Sewell Hall. I left my bike locked there and I don't need my parents picking up on this weed…" Kip nodded and steered right through the right fork in the road. He didn't see the runner and the runner didn't see him. It happened so fast. The runner bounced off the windshield as Rales screamed, "STOP!!!!!". The runner side somersaulted off the windshield landing on the right side of the street as Kip slammed on the brakes…

"Oh Christ! What just happened? Kip felt the blood rush to his face. Being the son of a lawyer, he knew this could change everything. Being the son of the Boulder County Prosecutor, it did in silent and unspoken ways he would struggle the rest of his life to untangle. He looked at Rennie and Rales. He just wanted to disappear. Rales said it first. "The asshole just ran in front of the car". They looked at each other for reassurance. Their glances in the rear view mirrors caught the pedestrians and students gathering around the runner lying unconscious in the dirt and gravel collected along the side of the street. Finding contrition and compunction in the haze, they rolled up the windows. They opened the doors and walked slowly back toward the gathering crowd.

"What happened?" blurted a young professor type pondering suspiciously the three friends. Rales reinforced the instant memory and traumatic file, "he just ran in front of the car —it's like he never even looked". The young professor found a familiar face from the French Dept. office staff. "Monique, did you see what happened?" She shook her head. "Not really, just as the brakes screeched and he landed". Still unconscious, an ambulance squealed in the far distance. "Who called 911?" offered one of the bystanders. Everyone looked around and shrugged shoulders in quick succession. Kip remembered overhearing his Dad's retelling how suspects spoke when they shouldn't or didn't need to…he said nothing as he stared at the unconscious runner breathing heavily.

Just as the ambulance pulled forward of the body and backed up toward it, a Boulder cop pulled over behind the crowd staring at the body. The EMT motioned the onlookers to back away as he set his equipment next to the fallen runner. "He's breathing…let Memorial know we're coming with a pedestrian struck hard by a car". Kip froze as he heard the words. "Struck hard by a car" carried a meaning not lost on him. He hit this guy. Not the other way around—innocence this time would require some creativity. The policeman settled on the three friends standing off to the side, "who was driving… who's car is it?"

Quietly, Kip pulled his wallet from his hip pocket and sled the Colorado drivers license and proof of insurance from the clear sleeve. Handing them over, "the car belongs to my dad". As the cop looked up from the license, he pointed at the insurance card. "This is your dad?" In an even lower tone, Kip conceded "yes, I'm Kip Jager". Few people in the crowd realized how much communication just occurred.

In just a few days, Kip would need to leave for his junior year at Virginia. He missed Raleigh when the summers came to an end. Still, he loved being away from Boulder for school. Growing up in a college town, he just needed to leave. This time, it might not be so easy. The Boulder cop watched everyone and saw the contrite look on Kip's face. Knowing that Kip's dad was the District Attorney created an unavoidable affinity. They all looked after one another.

Plus, the DA owing a cop a favor could come in very handy. No one seem to witness the accident. When a second officer began to separately question Rennie and a third female officer questioned Raleigh, the story still seemed to hang together. The car headed through the right fork and the runner ran directly in front of the right fender. Clipped mid-stride, the runner would be lucky to land on the hood, windshield and roadside. Under the station wagon, he'd been a goner.

What no one knew except for Kip? He'd been on the left side of the lane expecting to bear left down the hill. When Rennie changed his mind, the runner had already looked away and started across the right hand fork in the road. Kip turned right and didn't see the runner under the shade of the trees lining University Avenue. In that split second of changing directions with the car, the runner has already checked the direction of Kip's car. That split second changed two lives..

Still, the officer knew none of this detail. He considered that there might be a way to absolve everybody. After the ambulance took the runner to the Boulder Memorial emergency room, he gathered his notes and arrived not long before the runner began to regain consciousness. At this point, this student's girlfriend managed to work her way past the drape providing some privacy. He suspected trouble as he sized her up.

Cooly, he wrote out the traffic citation which charged the runner with "crossing at other than an intersection". Then, he marked the location of the accident as the intersection of University and 16th Street. That should do it. The DA's office would owe the officer a favor. Any reasonable judge would dismiss the ticket—a hearing he would plan on not attending.

As he taped the ticket to the bed sheet, the girlfriend inhaled and offered an expletive all in one motion. "Are you fucking kidding me? Boulder High kids joyriding and you ticket him? Are you crazy?". Officer Birch let her have it. "One more word out of you, and YOU'RE going downtown. Leaving her with a stunned expression, he strode out the side door to his squad car and the task of finishing his paperwork.

Kip knew enough to call Dad from home. He already knew. In the back and forth on the police radio, a detective walked down to Alex Jager's office to tell him that something was up and sounded ominous. By the time Officer Birch returned to the County Justice Center, staff members slowly heard the news. The DA's son hit a CU student jogging on a Friday afternoon. Ticketing the student didn't seem that out of the ordinary. They were all a bunch of rich space cadets to many of the locals. The student probably wasn't paying any attention. For Kip, all of these outside considerations just added to the confusion. This began a change in the arc of his life. A sense that the rules did not apply to him became almost unavoidable.

Kip planned to take the Law School Acceptance Test in the spring. Law school began to seem like a shrewd career choice for a guy who seemed to regularly bump up against life's guard rails. Maybe he could litigate against drivers of cars and trucks who caused accidents that only monetary compensation could help alleviate. Karma can be easily rationalized. Somehow it quieted the grimace in his mind when he imagined himself punishing negligent drivers for their carelessness. It just seemed so right. Strum Law School at the University of Denver agreed and accepted Kip two years later, and so it began.

How life played out for the jogger, now that would be a very different story.

27

Boulder Strikes

The shouting—"Get that woman outta here!"—jarred me back to consciousness. The first thing I saw was the ceiling of the emergency room; the next was the nurse, looking at me like I was a guilty prisoner.

Wait a minute, what was going on here?

I remember running along the sidewalk next to Varsity Pond—a Friday afternoon four-miler. I was getting a little extra conditioning before the start of the fall season.

Then, I kind of remember the inside of the ambulance. Now I was on my back in an emergency room. I heard a doctor say, "He needs that leg x-rayed" and reached down to touch my left knee. I felt gravel and blood, and the nurse firmly placed my hand back up on my chest, on top of the bed sheet. I could taste blood at the side of my mouth.

The police officer went back to writing out the traffic ticket and finished by taping it to my bed. At that point, my girlfriend really lost it.

"Are you fucking kidding me?" Ann screamed. "Boulder High kids joyriding and you ticket him? Are you crazy?"

The cop had enough. "One more word outta you, and you're going downtown."

On the phone to my parents, Ann's reaction reflected her usual smooth, measured style of communication: "His

face is just, just… gone," she told my mother thoughtlessly. Fortunately, my mom was used to Ann's penchant for drama and hyperbole. Ann shared ancestry with ancient Scottish warriors and with Chaldean Christians from Syria who had successfully fought their way from Damascus to Detroit. A measured reaction was simply not in her arsenal.

This was my welcome to the University of Colorado. Classes hadn't started yet. Summer was winding down, and making the CU soccer team had been a very close call. After two and a half weeks of practice, it was obvious that the coach favored the foreign players. They WERE better. But given that Detroit seemed like a foreign country to most Coloradans, he reluctantly kept me on the squad. Extra conditioning seemed like a necessity. The altitude alone made it a good idea.

My preferred training path took me to the upper entrance to Chautauqua Park, down to Ninth Street, and then back to University Avenue as it turned into Sixteenth Street near Boulder High. At the bend of University into Sixteenth, a side street forks toward Sewell Hall and Old Main. Running, I had looked west on University. The station wagon on the left looked like it would stay in its lane, so I kept running. Nope. After I looked away, it headed up the side street and struck me at the intersection. Providentially, the car hit my fibula in mid stride. A nanosecond later, it cracked my tibia. Thirty years later, I would learn that somersaulting into the windshield fractured my hip. The last roll off the side of the car included dragging my face, skin and knees through the gravel gathered below the curb of the street.

Marking my crime as "crossing at other than an inter-section" was this officer's first mistake. His second mistake was marking the ticket as occurring at the intersection of University and Sixteenth. This one really raised some eyebrows, particularly as the judge pondered how the student on crutches, with gauze around his face, could be the one charged.

His advice to me, "Kid, find out who was driving that car. Not guilty," he stated simply.

Fair enough. One call by my attorney to the Boulder County Justice Center revealed the driver to be none other than Kip Jager, son of Boulder County Prosecutor Alex Jager.

Sweet Jesus!

That kid would carry a set of traumatic files around in his mind for a long time. I was lucky to be walking, but so would I. That's karma in a world of automobiles and shady police officers. With a different father, he'd be in a heap of trouble.

No investigation ever occurred. He simply never was called to account. Unfortunately, this karma hung heavily on Kip throughout his own life. Plagued by a rocky 25 year marriage that ended in widely publicized divorce, soon afterward, he endured the tragic drug-induced suicide of his twenty year old son.

Transferring to CU from Wesleyan seemed like an odd decision to my friends and family. Some approved of my romance with Ann. Most didn't. Five years older than me, she seemed to have a hold on me that worried my family—particularly my mother. Ann possessed a forceful personality and typically got her way. Whether it was the race riot she nearly ignited in high school, her own decision to transfer from Michigan to Colorado, or her hold on her boyfriends, she rarely deferred to anyone. Being younger, I didn't stand a chance. Bottom line—my parents cut me off financially when I left Wesleyan for CU.

On my own, working at Pelican Pete's seafood restaurant, I managed to make ends meet without taking on too much student debt. This pedestrian car accident set me back, but not permanently. However, being sexually involved with Ann, who was five years older seemed fraught with emotional and psychological peril. Saying no to an older, more powerful woman had been made harder by that nasty babysitter. Eventually, I summoned up the courage to break up with Ann. Even I could only take so much manipulation. I'd had my fill.

The Boulder Police Department had also had their fill of my brothers at the Alpha Psi Delta Lodge. Situated at the triple intersection of Broadway, College, and Fourteenth Street, the Lodge took college high jinks to profoundly stupid levels. You wouldn't believe what an oxygenated, flaming foam couch looks like in a thirty-two-foot free fall, unless you'd seen it for yourself. Ours was initially reported as a meteor sighting, an impression corrected only when the officer called to investigate disgustedly responded to base:

"Negative on the meteor sighting. It's a couch loaded with doobies."

Fraternity life wasn't all stupid mindless pranks. I did acquire some collegiate knowledge. Learning how to sneak a keg of beer into the football stadium, for example—that requires real skill:

- Procure a wheelchair.
- Sit a brother with a lower plate of fake teeth into that wheelchair.
- Place shop glasses on his face.
- Ask him to drool with his fake teeth ajar.
- Place the pony keg under the wheelchair.
- Cover him with a blanket—ideally one featuring our mascot, Ralphie the buffalo.
- Voila! You can now serve your classmates copious amounts of ice cold Coors while watching our beloved Buffs get drilled by Billy Sims and the Oklahoma Sooners. Coors: the beer to have when you're only having eleven.

The real Ralphie greeted the Sooners with an appropriate welcoming present that day. After being run onto the field by her "handlers"—at a thousand pounds, believe me: she "handled" them—she stopped just short of the tunnel where she normally ran back into her trailer. The sight of the Oklahoma Sooners dressed in their all-white visitors' uniforms may have spooked her. Nonetheless, she laid down a buffalo pie roughly the size of the "C" and "O" in the "Colorado" painted across the north end zone. Served 'em right: shame on the Sooners for trying to scare the shit out of our beloved Ralphie.

The brotherhood's relations with Boulder's finest became significantly worse with the end of semester. The Lodge had a ten-year history of setting things on fire, and this preoccupation with localized arson flared after finals. Our pyre of abandoned furniture, crates, and boxes turned our front yard into a boozy communal bonfire. The police arrived at the scene of this latest infraction with two squad cars. When they falsely accused our president, Ron Osbourne, of staging the whole light show, things became very tense. Happily ensconced in his room doing his engineering homework, Ronnie had contributed not one idea or piece of abandoned furniture to the evening's festivities. When the cop walloped him in the sternum with his flashlight, an irrational moment of vengeance—spurred, no doubt, by months of charged memories and repressed anger—brought my right fist across the officer's jaw. PROBLEM! Not even knowing what I'd done, my buddies squirreled me upstairs until threats of multiple arrests finally brought me downtown to remand myself to the authorities.

This time, I had no girlfriend to scream the cops into distraction. I would be heading to the pokey—no ifs, ands or buts. Luckily, I hadn't broken his jaw; unfortunately, I had shattered his patience—along with that of the rest of the police force. Only one thing saved me: My attorney remembered the individual who had mowed me down and sent me to the Boulder Hospital emergency room. "You drop this charge," he said smoothly, "and we'll drop ours."

Karma can be damn divine. So can the justice that plagues the subrational mind.

Years later, I spent some time with a corporate shrink. She poked around my issues with false accusations stemming from the death of Jan Nunley and the ugly babysitter. She called my attention to the notably prickly response I had written to an innocuous email about my activity and expense reports. Geez, these folks don't miss much. This email (and a few other episodes) earned me three days of verbal volleyball with a professionally trained traumatologist, a mental health professional well-versed in the psychological jujitsu required to pull up charged memories and help the traumatized mind consider them at a healthy distance.

At first, the process seemed laborious.

"Okay, let's repeat that event and shorten it to a moment."

"Please repeat it, but shorten up the time frame."

After reliving what had happened over and over and over, it suddenly hit me. I was damn lucky. I could have been in jail. I could have been in a wheelchair. I was lucky just to be alive.

Life can be so tragic. Yet here I am, writing about this wild ride of a life. You can't make this shit up. After repeating and rinsing a few times, the emotions dry up. The files, released of their charge, go back into your mental file drawer. You're clear…one file at a time.

Post-traumatic Growth

Research carried out in 2013 by Harvard's H'Sien Hayward indicates that paralyzed accident survivors might actually enjoy levels of happiness equal—or slightly higher—to those of lottery winners. On the surface, this seems counterintuitive. But as Dr. Hayward points out, "A traumatic event shakes you up." No doubt. This timely research emerges around a new term, "post-traumatic growth."

Maybe a sense of purpose can, in fact, originate in these traumatic setbacks. Peace and serenity come from a healthy balance of mind, body, and spirit, and maybe these traumas strengthen our spirit. Maybe it's the spirit—that sense of purpose in our life—that deserves our attention.

As crazy and traumatic as Boulder and Grand Bahama seemed when looking back, they helped me to grow and get on with learning how to handle life's setbacks. My playing days ended with that car striking me, but it wasn't long before I started coaching youth soccer and finding new ways to give back. I concentrated on my studies and completed a degree in economics in just three years. Starting work less than a month after commencement in Boulder, I managed to enjoy a thirty-two-year career in the investment industry.

I do carry baggage from the accident—related, as that corporate psychologist pointed out, to a fear of being falsely accused or not believed. Yet, with the help of a supportive family and a friend trained as a traumatologist, I continued working on my own case. In time, those charged memories began to lighten in number and intensity. The search for a way to clear these episodes never completely stops, but you learn to revisit them at an increasing distance and with greater clarity and perspective.

Seeing the irrationality in myself actually opened up my ability to see it in others. Just as I recognized my own tendency to dwell too much on previous "wins" as a way of avoiding re-engagement with new challenges, I see much more clearly how others do the same thing. Friends who alienate themselves can help remind me how, at times, I pull back and prefer solitude—perhaps a little too much. Nowhere does this show up more than when I watch the various political debates.

Living through the demise of Detroit and Grand Bahama leaves me pretty cynical about grandiose government planning schemes. Yet, as I write these stories, I see Bernie Sanders on television, gaining ground as a candidate for President. He seems pretty rational, absent the "charge" of many of the other candidates. I'm pretty sure that his policies won't work, but I don't worry about him as a person. He seems to have his head on straight.

I think back to leaders like FDR, JFK, and Ronald Reagan. Maybe their charisma stemmed, in part, from the traumas of their younger days. FDR, overcoming his polio, looks very uplifting in light of this research and perspective. Losing an older brother to war, and barely surviving himself, Jack Kennedy would be a good example of posttraumatic growth.

Ronald Reagan, tasked with rising above the poverty and alcoholism of his father, developed a sunny optimism that radiated through his speeches and his leadership.

Like many of us, old traumas may still chill me; however, the lessons I've learned warm me to the core. Lessons taken from the basement of time and offered up to generations not yet born.

Each of us has a story that can still be written—a story that only we get to write.

28

Unlucky Lot

Fengshui tells us building your home across the street from a church leads to bad luck. Grandma loved that lot on Hendrie Boulevard. She admired the stately neighborhood. The church seemed warm. It all looked like the American Dream to her. Now try this on for size, after my grandfather and great uncle bought that lot, built a fine home and moved the family; little uncle Stevie briefly met his Maker, mesothelioma struck my grandmother, and mom married dad in that very church. Christ all Friday, this fengshui might just not be a bunch of happy horse fertilizer…

Uncle Stevie loved speed. At ten years old, he would sit in the front seat of the family car while my mom would drive and time her with a stop watch as the traffic light turned green from red. Urging her to step on it, faster and quicker. Stevie loved speed like tigers enjoy chow time. The faster you could go, the better. The only thing worse than a gear head in Michigan? A mechanical gear head who could make bikes and cars go faster and faster. He was always ready to test them. It all caught up to him one clear, sunny summer afternoon.

The elderly man earned his driver's license at an older age. When he graduated from high school, cars still seemed like a novelty. Even in Michigan, learning to drive for many came at an adult age. This poor fellow even voluntarily retook the driving test when the optometrist prescribed new eyeglasses. The neighborhood around Hendrie Boulevard offered broad swathes of shade over the streets and sidewalks. The elms and oaks stood that high and mighty. Still, in the shadows, the intersections could alternate suddenly from long afternoon light to sunny glare. One element to this micro drama and trauma trumped all others.

Stevie was long and lean with strong legs. He could pump that Schwinn to over thirty miles per hour. 30 mph on M-1 seems slow. 30 mph on a sidewalk and into an intersection happens faster than an heartbeat. The elderly man driving the car didn't have a chance. Stevie came down the sidewalk ramp into Hendrie Boulevard at full throttle. If only he had hit the side of the elderly man's car. No, he came right in front of it just as it came even with the sidewalk. Two objects both moving at speeds over 30 mph do not collide well. The elderly man had the engine, hood and front grille to protect him. Little Stevie had only his forehead.

First, the car ran over the bike. Then, it ran over Stevie who had been thrown off the bike.

His forehead broke into so many pieces, some were too small for the surgeons to see. Some were closer to his left ear than his left eye. For over an hour, the surgeons stood over little Stevie trying almost everything to save him. Finally, the lead surgeon quietly stepped back from the table, removed his surgical gloves, washed his hands, and strode through the emergency room door to speak to my grandparents. He realized immediately that he was speaking only to Big Maggie. She was in charge—in charge of her family, her school classrooms, this doctor, this hospital, and maybe ONLY not her own demons.

The surgeon compassionately and solemnly informed Big Maggie that, "nothing more can be done…call in your minister". Big Maggie looked at this man with an eye that can only be described as a mixture of disdain and pity. "Their job is to save his soul. Your job is to save his life." Whereupon, she literally grabbed the doctor by the upper arm and launched him back into the emergency room. Big Maggie didn't like quitters.

An hour earlier, the surgeons had briefly considered a procedure that would lead to putting a prosthetic plate in place of what had been Stevie's forehead. The returning surgeon reluctantly stated flatly, "let's give it a try". Three hours later, they had stitched his head back together. Three weeks later, Stevie sort of woke up. Thirteen months later, he returned to school with a permanent wink on his forehead. Thirteen years later he was accepted to medical school from Michigan State University. It wasn't U of M. But for a guy with a titanium plate for a forehead, it was probably the most the family could expect. We decided to give him a pass.

A few years later, Steve accepted a position as a research scientist with Merck in South San Francisco. What I remember most vividly? He owned a Goodwood (Spartan) Green 1967 Corvette convertible. He bought one with the 427 cubic inch engine and 430 plus horsepower. Some of those cars generated so much horsepower, GM didn't publish an actual horsepower reading. They feared the insurance industry wouldn't insure the car. Stevie added aluminum alloy piston heads with forged pistons coupled to a solid lifter camshaft. Insurers might have been exactly right had they known how Steve tinkered with her at night. This baby personified speed. The NASA astronauts loved those Corvette years.

The last time I saw that car, it had nearly 400,000 miles on it. It owned the highways in a Northern Nevada. It was the love of his life.

Big Maggie stood even taller after willing her son Steve back to life. She lived in a home she admired, in a neighborhood which made her proud, and her daughter attended the University of Michigan. Life had begun very poorly for

Maggie. Yet, she eventually made her way out of the white trash west side of Detroit and Warren Avenue. Those modest homes and dusty streets fueled her imagination and ambition. Supported by older siblings financially and with housing, she attended the University in Ann Arbor, graduating in 1926. She eventually became a successful and well respected high school teacher of Latin and history. She'd come a long way. She may not have found happiness, but she had found good fortune. Then, out of the blue, disaster struck.

Asbestos came into the lining of American's lungs from many sources. Navy shipyards blew asbestos as insulation. Homes used it similarly. Roof shingles needed the durability asbestos provided. People didn't. It was everywhere working people labored and loved. Women married to such workers breathed in asbestos specks every time they washed their husband's clothes, or their own.

Big Maggie married grandpa knowing he earned valedictorian honors in high school. Too shy to give the valedictory speech, he asked if he could be salutatorian instead. This guy was perfect for Big Maggie. Smart enough to keep up with her, too shy to argue with her. Once he joined Uncle Emil in his sheet metal and roof building company, the die was cast. He'd carry bundles of shingles over his shoulder as he climbed the ladders up to the roof structures of the buildings they built. Those asbestos specks made their way into his shirts and the knees of his work pants. Eventually, they made their way into the laundry that Big Maggie washed at home. Baking inside her lungs, those specks made their way with each of her breathes out to the lining of her lung. Some called it "pleurisy". Others called lung cancer. To be precise, it was cancer of the LINING of the lung. Diagnosed with a condition we now know as mesothelioma while her daughter attended college in Ann Arbor, Big Maggie didn't have much time, nor did the family she ran like a Baptist church service.

One evening, mom intuitively knew after dinner with her aunt and uncle to go to the University Hospital. A young intern sprung the news on her as she approached her mother's hospital room. Fortunate to have her childhood friend Pat with her in Ann Arbor, she processed the news of her mother's final passing with a deep sense of anger. Big Maggie died on Little Maggie's twentieth birthday. This would be complicated.

Tightness across my mother's face told me that what she was about to share would be difficult. Her eyes moistened as she described the beatings she absorbed from my grandmother's open and clenched hand. Big Maggie told Little Maggie it would "improve" her. Sometimes, the mind's ability to rationalize will drop your jaw.

Grandma was a carrier. She endured a very rough up-bringing being the youngest of six as the poor daughter of a heavy drinker. Receiving more than her fair share of angry outbursts and physical abuse, she passed those onto Little Maggie. At precisely the same age, Big Maggie began to use her hands not to hug and console. She told Little Maggie plainly that these beatings were to "take the devil out you". "They're good for your soul".

This abuse probably created the same fear, confusion and shame that my grandmother as a child could not under-stand or process as the receiver. Unable to understand how a loved one can be so charged and irrational, these young minds cannot parse out or reason through such behavior. Even cast in religious terms, it makes no sense. Big Maggie's older sisters actively considered removing Little Maggie from the home. Grandpa intervened and promised to protect her. He did the best he could.

Children of parents who physically abuse them cannot be blamed for hoping their parents die. When they do actually die, the guilt can be paralyzing. We all know instinctively to love our parents. When that becomes difficult or virtually im-possible, confusion fuses into shame and the receiver becomes bottled up with guilt. Big Maggie buried her father at age ten. Little Maggie would bury Big Maggie at age twenty.

Family members thought Little Maggie to be shy. It was so much more than that. She was afraid. Afraid of being hit hard, mocked and ridiculed, Little Maggie could go nowhere with her anger, humiliation and shame. Big Maggie's death shook her daughter to the core.

Friends tell me that mom went weeks without speaking more than a few words and eating more than a few forkfuls. A young woman free of the abuse she'd received for years, the guilt at having her darkest hope come true meant being as secretive as possible. Except for one single spontaneous loud, shrieking wail at Big Maggie's graveside, Little Maggie said as little as possible. One thing for sure, it was not the right time to fall in love.

Climbing over fellow students to find her seat in political science class, she brushed up against him. At nearly 6'3", he was lean and long. Dubbed by the professor, "our legal eagle", this law student needed to fill some undergraduate requirements after transferring to Michigan from the Virginia Military Institute. He became the new object for her pent up emotional energy. Although he noticed her, he didn't reciprocate. He didn't want the awkwardness of a one time date sitting near him for the rest of the semester. He waited until the last day of class.

"Would you like to go for some coffee?" Leaving out the front steps of Angell Hall, they headed up the sidewalk along State Street towards Drake's Sandwich Shop and Martian Tea Room on North University Avenue. Anachronistic and eccentric even in 1955, Drake's offered patrons order pads to write out their requests, and one of the most hideous combinations of mint green and black paint on their high back wooden booths. Plenty of privacy for the cooing co-eds, their coffee became a two hour deposition.

The ghost of Big Maggie loomed large. The legal eagle went by Don and "Donny" to his law school classmates, one of whom stopped by to spy on the pretty young co-ed enjoying coffee with his buddy. Little Maggie quickly deduced that Donny enjoyed an occasional bourbon. Right there, mom had her first small chunk of revenge. Big Maggie banned alcohol and any dates who were suspected of such wicked, sinful conduct. Little Maggie was ready to learn to drink. "Our legal eagle" seemed like the perfect sandy haired, blue-green eyed, responsible mentor to open up a new world of sophistication and sin.

Courting Little Maggie proved more fun than Donny anticipated. Free of her harsh master, mom could start to play at life without fear of admonishment and censure. Nowhere better to play than among the law school fraternity brothers living along Ann Arbor's Hill Street. She could be anyone she imagined. After a few martinis, she fended off one pesky aspiring attorney by telling him her name was "Lisa Dominique" —an exchange student from the south of France. She and Don laughed over coffee at hearing of the poor guy's futile efforts in the Registrar's Office at tracking down the visiting scholar from Cannes.

Courtship included long weekends studying together in the family homes and cottages around Crystal Lake and Elberta. Donny loved "up north" as Michiganders like to say. He'd never before seen the sand dunes, harbor towns and ancient meadows along the sunset shore of Lake Michigan. He was smitten.

Ultimately, both Little Maggie and Donny made similar decisions. These clever, resourceful and attractive young lovers would, in time, become a different kind of person. They would become good parents; loving, supportive and never prone to striking or mistreating a child. If the American Dream centers on giving children a better life than you had, Donny and Maggie wed full of confidence. They wed in that church across the street from that unlucky lot.

Observing a marriage from the vantage point of eldest child, impartial objective assessments come slowly, only with years of maturity and perspective. Great marriages seem to ferment in companionship, laughter, playful intimacy and years of shared experiences. A mother deeply into the books of Ayn Rand and Sigmund Freud seems a poor match for an outdoorsman always shooting a pheasant, casting a trout fly, and striking a golf ball. The shared memories just leave behind too many lonely gaps. For Maggie and Donny, rational and realistic assessments like these were made difficult by the timing of their courtship.

Donny carried the uncleared emotions and considerations created by killing the intoxicated man staggering in front of his car on a rainy foggy night. Maggie needed years of counsel to unravel the harsh cords of anger and shame striking at her child mind. Only a few years after these heavy memories followed such untimely deaths, they wed in that church across the street from that unlucky lot. An unlucky lot jarring the lives of the very people who trespassed upon it.

Securing Your Life Mask

A sixteen year marriage can be extended until the kids graduate from high school. Or, it can be cut short so both adults move on with life. Donny chose the latter and tried to pin it on mom. It didn't work. Mostly, she secured her own life mask. The quality of her life improved steadily.

During the later years in the Bahamas, mom and dad dropped us off at school and drove to the beach. They enjoyed playing chess on the beach. I heard that they rarely wore clothes. Life for them became a bit sybaritic and leisurely. In time, dad decided that traveling back and forth to Florida was too much hassle by commercial jet or a boat. He decided he would learn to fly, and eventually buy a plane.

Mom heard about this idea and realized this would be her way to make her childhood dream of being a female Charles Lindbergh a reality.

"Don, if you become a pilot, maybe I should take a few lessons in case something happens to you inside the cockpit of the plane. Just as a precaution…"

Dad nodded. "Yeah, that's probably a good idea."

She had her chance.

She passed every test. She passed every exam. Even when her single engine plan lost power, she managed a dead stick (prop not moving) landing. Plus, during this dead stick landing, instead of interfering with the Eastern Airlines 727 bearing down behind her on the same runaway, she landed her plane in the grassy area to the right of the actual runaway. She could not only fly a plane. She could fly really well under real pressure.

Dad couldn't pass all of the aviation exams or tests. Eventually, he gave up on earning his pilot's license. At that point, their differences began to mean something. Mom began to move beyond Don. She took over more and more control of her life. She began to own her decisions in a conscious and rational way. Don continued to just react. Worse, he couldn't see his self-defeating behavior. It was subconscious and irrational.

Dad asked for the divorce. I'm not sure he even knew why he wanted it. He reacted mournfully to the death of his dad, Grandpa Don with a running series of trysts and affairs. Grandpa's death left a huge, gaping hole in his life. Mom grew weary of him clumsily trying to fill it.

When mom and dad began negotiating the details of the divorce, dad preferred to keep all the assets and pay a basic alimony. Instinctively, mom knew that arrangement was a bad idea. At first, the idea of a monthly legally mandated check seemed attractive. As they negotiated and argued, trust began to slip away. Once she lost a sense of trust, she needed a new solution.

Mom didn't like debt. It added to her anxiety and frustration with dad. He was a real estate owner, operator and promoter. For him, debt was like oxygen. He used it all the time. He became numb to its downside. Oxygen poisoning seemed a far off problem. Mom knew better.

She simply said to the divorce mediator that she'd take the two apartment complexes with the lowest mortgage balances and $100,000 in cash. Dad could keep the other dozen complexes and the rest of the liquid assets. Presto, divorce agreement reached. They parted ways in 1975.

Mom says she made every mistake an inexperienced owner could make…once. She collected rents but used a resident manager as a daily presence on the properties. She collected laundry tokens. She planted flowers. When the nearby college built a new intramural athletic complex and HVAC equipment directly on her property line and adjacent units, she used her moxie. A local ordnance mandated that a noise complaint begin with a call to the police. She organized her tenants to a schedule of calling the police every time the HVAC motor cranked up to start. After a week the police couldn't take it anymore. They told the college to stop the noise violations or they'd be ticketed and fined. Problem solved.

Over 26 years, she managed expenses, increased rents and paid off the mortgages. Her cash flow rose slowly but steadily. Finally, in 2001 when she was ready to retire, she sold them.

Using her sons' familiarity with the American Funds mutual fund family to her ultimate advantage, she rolled her capital gains into a very, very comfortable blue chip standard of living. Although she never remarried, she secured her own life mask. She fully became her own person. She never looked back again at that unlucky lot on Hendrie Boulevard. It cast a long spell on her family. She stepped out of that dark spell.

29

You're Not Jewish?

S itting at my cubicle as a 21 year old trainee in the company's management training program made me a bit of a sitting duck. That can be both good and bad. Our leader and managing partner, Jerry Reinsdorf would walk in every morning with a briefcase specifically designed for a guy who wanted to bring home a ton of a work and avoid spending too much time actively listening to his wife. It was a double wide. Occasionally, he'd offer a smiling good morning to the young staff. Other times, his face could be a little tight.

After raising a lot of money from political donors for the reelection of Democrats, he still was not a fan of President Jimmy Carter. His post mortem greeting hit the nail on the head. "It's as if the country just took a long trip to the commode…" Other mornings, his practical joker side could catch you a little off stride:

"You're not Jewish?" he probed gently.

After looking around to see if his question was meant for someone else, I offered.

"Ah, no actually I'm not…"

"You look Jewish?"….

I shrugged my shoulders.

"We thought you were Jewish when we hired you…"

Double shoulder shrug.

Finally, the best I had at 7:30 in the morning.

"How Jewish do I need to be…?"

"Nah, you're fine, get back to work…"

Such was my indoctrination to the most politically in-correct, mind expanding and super bright group of business partners to grace the world of real estate investing.

In the early 1980's, the exodus from the upper Midwest to the Sun Belt gathered steam with the election of Reagan and the two major tax reforms that the Democratic majorities helped him pass. Our firm became active both in the southeast and the southwest. Some of our finest investments came in the area known as the "Research Triangle". One local developer became our joint venture partner in Durham, Chapel Hill, Greensboro and Raleigh, North Carolina.

Essentially, our cutting edge structures turned our "equi-ty" into a stream of largely deductible interest payments known as soft dollars. Understanding the tax code like the Talmud, Jerry and his partners attracted investors and real estate part-ners in droves. I tagged along for the first deal with this North Carolina developer, so this trip became a real eye-opener. Let's just say a Boston Red Sox fan would call our deal structure wicked smart.

The culture clash of a clever Jewish northern attorney and the bulldog smart UNC law grad was palpable. Our struc-ture was complex, subtle and shifted the financial risk to this local partner. We would not be leaving until this Chapel Hill attorney fully understood AND explained the full extent of this deal to his client.

Because review of the deal began to drag on and on, the local developer decided to give us a tour of some future, potential building sites. When we returned, he received quite a shock from his Tar Heel lawyer. Not only did this lawyer explain how we were turning our equity into tax deductible soft dollars, his role as local developer would put virtually all of the short term bank risk onto his balance sheet. His face belied his reaction.

He stared at the numbers, dates and arrows on the white board. He looked at his attorney intently as he asked a few questions. He looked at our acquisitions director and our smart Yankee lawyer. He exhaled long and hard.

"This is the deal we made?" he asked looking over to our side of the table.

We simply nodded.

"If that's the deal we made, I will honor it..." This old-school southern gentleman stood up and walked out of the conference room. He didn't stop to look back and say goodbye.

Our team knew we'd won that battle. But there would be more battles down the road. We'd better be ready.

One last errand before I moved out of the management training program. Jerry had successfully negotiated the purchase of our local professional baseball team and its stadium, a venerable old collection of rafters in the rough part of town. Somehow, just as Jerry heats up the negotiation with the former owner, stories begin to appear in the local newspapers that the rival bidder actually wants to turn the Chicago White Sox into the New Orleans White Sox. Sports reports begin describing this rival's interest in the Louisiana Downs horse racing operations. Local sports fans begin to connect the dots. Move the team and more racing days will be allocated to this rival bidder. Let's just say the rival won the bidding, but lost the vote of the league owners.

Jerry's assistant Sherri calls me on the intercom and asks if I'm still driving the rusted out 1970 canary yellow Ford Country Squire Station Wagon? Having bought it for a cool $250 from a school teacher in Findlay, Ohio—it was one of my few actual assets. Sherri essentially filled the role of company cheerleader, mascot and police Sargent. She kept a solid finger on the pulse of the company. You didn't trifle with her. She was like a warm Jewish mother and beat cop all rolled into one radiant smile.

Sheepishly, I say "yes, yes, I am".

"Perfect! Please come up to our office. We have an errand for you."

"We need you to get the remaining subscription agreements for our baseball limited partnership signed and pick up the investor checks. We prepared a crib sheet of possible Q&A.

Here is the list of investors and their addresses. They expect to see you this afternoon."

Well, this type of thing doesn't happen everyday. I remember being nervous as hell. Still, it seemed like a chance to earn a stripe or two with the partners of the firm. Many of them had already decided to invest and own a small piece of the team.

The deal structured for the investors was sophisticated and clever beyond words. All of the most advanced tax treatments for player contracts and stadium assets would be included. The new scoreboard would be carved out for separate accounting, and the exterior facade of baseball's oldest stadium would be donated to the historical society as a charitable contribution.

This advanced financial creativity would change and help to save baseball. Initially, it saved baseball for the south side of Chicago. In time, all the teams employed variations of this artful finance. Jerry was on his way to being a quiet, very influential baseball owner. All by the book, but the IRS code book was one that few actually read. Jerry read it. He read it thoroughly. It was one hell of a deal.

My job was simple errand running. With the press following our leader everywhere, my rusty yellow Ford was perfect cover. My tour of the Jewish hoi paloi began at the iconic Hancock Tower on Michigan Avenue. The owners of our real estate rivals delegated this paperwork process to their attorney John Brooklyn. Next, I met Bob Lurie who also had a very successful real estate investment firm, and helped run the Gravedancer Fund. Lurie loved the deal. Another confident smart investor found his way into the ownership of the

Chisox. Next, I visited the president and owner of the local professional soccer team. Lastly, I found the office of "H. Rosenthal—Commodities Broker".

A simple steel door with frosted glass guarded a dimly lit office. You could describe this business as low in overhead and high in profitability. Walking into this one room square office, I was greeted by a secretary who was a dead ringer for Miss Hathaway on the television show *"Beverly Hillbillies"*, the one who worked for the bank president, Mr. Drysdale. She had mastered the demur short haircut parted from the back of her head. It was as if Jane Kulp retired from television and was hired by old Rosenthal himself. Mr. Rosenthal could only be described as a Jewish leprechaun. With two old style cradle phones balanced on each shoulder, he barked out orders, "buy pork bellies", into the other phone "short yen", into the opposite phone, "buy frozen orange juice", back again "short Deutsch marks". Into the middle of this bizarre scene, walks the official errand boy for the Chicago White Sox.

"You mas be Jerry's boy…." he began.

I introduced myself and sat down in front of him and his bank of computer screens.

"Zis a gaad deal?" began the Yiddish leprechaun.

"Well sir, we feel that while our structure covers new ground, the tax treatments are rooted in established case law and should hold". As I memorized and restated the crib sheet.

"Ya ya, but da bizness? Da numbers, how do dey look?" was his follow up. Meanwhile, he just processed another stack of trades from his head, "pork bellies, yen, OJ, francs".

It all seemed a bit surreal to a young trainee. Still, I was learning and soaking up everything I could. Outlining how the tax treatment allowed for the aggressive signing of new pitching and hitting stars, Rosenthal smiled at the image of a World Series on the old South Side.

Rosenthal then opens his ledger style business check book and calmly strokes one of the larger checks of any of the limited partners. It had a two, lots of zeroes and a comma or two.

As I left, I could still hear him. "Buy pork bellies, sell frozen orange juice…"

Not a day to be forgotten. I may not have converted to Judaism. However, I did owe these guys for the education of a lifetime. They built a business which employed thousands. Thousands of families directly benefited from their very authentic brand of enterprise. Business could be conducted in a tough unsentimental way and still leave you with a smile. Generous to family and friends, this tribe of business owners epitomize America and make us stronger. They give depth to this notion of diversity. They take it way beyond the shallow identity politics of today. They were very real. I was lucky to know them.

30

Voice of an Angel

The founding partners knew enough of American consumer attitudes to name their new firm something that sounded old English and "waspy". They liked Balfour but a college ring company took that name, so they settled on "Balcor". While enjoying some early successes, the leadership of Balcor decided in 1982 that, as a firm, all of us would go through a week long training to sharpen our public speaking and communication skills. To conduct the training we hired a particularly effective and empathetic instructor. Jennifer Lanza would turn out to be much more than a mere public speaking coach. Her recollections give detail and depth to what transpired that week.

As I initially settled into my particular communication workshop, one older woman who led our investor services department would clearly be slow to get on board with this new initiative. We began the workshop by each of us providing a short five minute background including where we grew up, our background, and our education. This lady spellbound us. Until that morning, we had no idea who Lily Edelman really was.

Born near Vienna, Austria in 1924, Lily's parents provided her with voice lessons once they heard her sing at a

Seder supper as a young girl. Clear and strong, her sweet voice covered a broad range and would captivate anyone listening. Once the Nazis arrived, her voice became her currency. A young German officer assigned to that section of Vienna heard her singing from down in the courtyard below her childhood home. His offer was a bit ambiguous but simple. Lily sang to him to stay alive and not be shipped north with her family. Her voice seem to cause her to "lose" her family and stay "alive". Her anger intensified as she recounted her short narrative. She said simply, "I've not sung since…"

Our oration workshop centered on Aristotle's triad of ethos, logos and pathos. How a communicator could touch an audience and move them to action. Ethos captured the need for the presenter to be credible by remaining authentic and connected to their essential character as a person in front of an audience. Don't try to fake it. Logos described how the reasons and proof for an argument must be coherent and sequential. Appeal to our sense of logic by presenting relevant facts and figures in a sensible order. Pathos strikes that emotional chord with the listener. Empathy and our need to care emotionally can move us to action as long as we don't feel manipulated or handled. Fertile ground for our Austrian Jewess as she reasoned herself through her own sense of character, memories and anger. Lily would go to that dark place that week of our workshop.

When you stand in front of a group of coworkers and present a new concept or idea, the mere nakedness of the moment exposes a person. For Lily, a full week of making short speeches took her to a new domain. It was as if the four or five minutes on her feet in front of us gave her a window into her own soul. Repetition of this act of revealing herself began to chip away and crack her mask of anger and resentment. Finally, on the third afternoon, while one on one with Lily in a separate training room, Jennifer chanced the question.

"Who are you most angry at…?"

"Angry? You mean me? Who am I most angry at?" Lily retorted.

After a long silence, "Is it that obvious?" Lily followed on inquisitively.

"Yes…it is." Jennifer answered.

She looked right through Lily giving her the time and space to compose her answer.

Her eyes weighed heavy with wet emotion, "myself" Lily said softly.

"If I hadn't gone down that path with the Germans, if I hadn't sang, I wouldn't have lost my parents."

Our quick trainer responded, "if you hadn't sang, you wouldn't be alive.."

"No, I wouldn't. But I wouldn't have lost mama, papa and my sister Magda. The pain is one and the same."

"Would you be willing to tell me your story?" Jennifer gently probed.

Lily looked right through Jennifer with her blue – green eyes. She murmured, "maybe…I'm not sure of everything anymore."

Finally, she nodded.

"This will take awhile. I'm not even sure where to start."

Jennifer returned her eye contact with clarity and comfort. "Start with what you first remember…".

Lily began. This would take the rest of the afternoon, and well into the evening.

VIENNA

"Music seemed everywhere around me from my earliest memory. I can remember my aunt Nicola at the piano, the small walnut grand in our sunroom. Of course, our papa performed as the second violinist in the Philharmonic, so he would play with mother or my aunt. It was usually after dinner. It's painful to remember. Remembering how beautiful they sounded. So pure, so clear."

She gently let her eyes moisten again as she recounted the old Yiddish songs and her parents' melodies.

"I haven't let myself remember those evenings in Vienna. It's been too much. It's been so much to lose…

"Wien as we citizens of Vienna remember her became an enclave for Jewish artists from Hungary and Germany. Mozart and Beethoven called it their home. Within Wien, Leopoldstadt became the Jewish quarter to many of our family and artists like those that performed with my father. Sabbath would be at Seitenstettengasse and music would continue at the Sabbath table after dinner. That's where we sang. That's the first time my parents heard me sing. It was late one evening as I harmonized with my grandmother and aunt. That's when my parents realized the voice God gave me.

Mimitzraim Gealtonu should be joyful and happy as it celebrates our exodus from Egypt. We would sing it as Viennese. We were proud. My voice instructor reminded me of our history. She explained our legacy. Singing to that legacy gave me joy. Thinking back, that's when my family knew of my voice, my gift. This gift that cost me my family."

"I can see my father standing behind my mother and aunt and their piano. He seemed so tall, so strong and yet silent. He would hold his violin under his chin. With straight back and firm carriage, only my aunt, maybe my grandmother would sing with me. Our voices could be so strong and clear. Us three, proud together…"

Tears started to stream as she tried to catch her breath.

"It never seemed possible that it would end. We were Austrians. We were Mendelssohns. We were not Germans. We knew who we were. Somehow, our pride made us vulnerable. We were so naive. We just couldn't see. When people envy what you have. Our homes, our music, our belongings…we just couldn't see the envy for what it was. What it really was…"

Jennifer stopped Lily at this point asking: "Envy, you say envy? What do you mean? How does envy explain any of this…this evil? Why do you call it envy?"

"I was young. I was a child. I think to myself now. These everyday people, Austrians, everyday Germans going about their jobs. Not thinking how their resentments and anti-Semitism could spiral out of control..."

'They wanted what we had. Our music was not recorded on a phonograph. We played it. We sang it. Our homes were filled with art and grace, and, most importantly, warmth. As family, we carved out a life for ourselves. We lived so well.'

These Nazis would come to neighbors' homes and just take their belongings. They rationalized all their bitterness and envy of us. Class warfare fused itself into our Jewishness.

Because my father was a prominente, we were among the last. Even after Freud left for London, we thought we had time. My aunt Nicola wanted us to leave for America. Father believed as a prominente, we would be left alone."

ANSCHLUSS

"Before the yellow stars and the graffiti on the shop glass, there was a vote. I was young. My parents kept saying that this vote would make things okay. The vote would mean the Germans would have to leave. Not close, not honest, not close at all. Austria voted for Hitler. It was so crazy. We voted for him! We voted for **him**! I think they just voted for revenge —to lash back at people who they thought caused their hard-

ships and challenges. At that point, the Germans would never leave."

"Germans like to march. Diz people *like to march*. They love flags and marching and making sure you can hear them and cannot ignore them.

Where did they all come from? They would come in the alleyways at night. They would come through the back doors of shops and offices. This vote made it seem like this craziness was okay."

As Lily wiped away the tears, she breathed in hurriedly. She asked so simply. "What else did we have? Only our music, we could play the songs and sing them...They could annex us, swallow us up. But they could not silence us...no, no. That they could not do."

Grand Bargain

"Sometimes I didn't even realize I was singing. During the summer, we would leave the windows open for the fresh air. In Leopoldstadt, warm smells from the bakeries and coffee shops filled our home. We lived above these shops. So crazy, the Germans would sit in these cafes and shops. You could hear their hard guttural high German. They were mostly from the north. It was there in their accent."

Lily would wave her hands at the craziness. These Germans invading her neighborhood. One German whose tight smile eventually betrayed a series of cunning motives seem to pick out Lily from the other Jews in the Leopoldstadt quarter.

"Du bist die sangerin?" asked the young German Sargent.

"Sangst du, 'Du bist die Ruhe'?" he seemed to know.

"This haunting song by Schubert, 'You are rest and peace' was a favorite of papa. It surprised me that a mere Sargent would even know this song. Really, it's a series of poems as a Lied. The song haunts you. It's so beautiful and profound and dark all at the same time."

Jennifer decided to move below Lily's assessments, and dive down into the undercurrents. She asked about the fragrances in the neighborhood through the open windows. She asked about the tastes of the food, the Seder and Passover meals. How her senses remembered those days before and just after the Anschluss. She wanted Lily to draw up her memory file in sensory form. Not just to describe and assess it, but to try to relive it.

"Must we go into such detail?" implored Lily.

"Trust me" said Jennifer simply. "It's more painful to keep this down so deep under the surface…trust me."

Lily began anew, "the Sargent seemed almost pleasant, not so stern like the other officers. I don't know for sure that he was a Nazi. Sometimes, it was hard to tell. Prurient images may have filled his mind, but not his face. His gaze would linger for too long, almost becoming a leer. He wore the uniform of the Wehrmacht, not a Brownshirt or SS. He looked ominous and cunning at the same time. His revulsion at my Jewishness bordered on obsession. I acknowledged that my voice did come from the open window above this patisserie. I told him the melody came from me, my grandmother and my aunt. I remembered his faint and insincere smile. It still seemed a mystery how this hardened Sargent would know Schubert and request such a song. It seemed so curious. That forced smile could only camouflage his menacing heart for so long."

Jennifer smiled. She could sense the traumatic confusion before Lily even outlined it.

"This young German asked if I would sing for him and his Captain. I hesitated. The idea seemed awful. Worse, it seemed dangerous. Where would this be? An office? A barracks? I shuttered at the idea of it all. I guess I began to worry about saying 'yes', as much as saying 'no'.

"Still it seemed that saying 'no' might be worse. Initially, he did seem a little bit pleasant, not like the Brownshirts. He knew music. He knew Schubert and this beautiful but obscure song. Maybe I just wanted to rationalize a way to say 'yes'. She hesitated by thanking him for the compliment.

"Let me ask my parents." Seemed the best way to stall the young Sargent. He smiled at her. My Captain takes his tea in the afternoon at 4:00. He brought his harpsichord piano. Do you play? Is that someone in your family playing the piano?"

"My aunt...my aunt Nicola", countered Lily.

"Please invite her as well. It would be quite nice...", the young Sargent almost seemed sincere...almost.

An innocuous admonition came with equal sincerity.

"You sing for us, the Captain will make things safe for you...safe for your aunt as well."

Lily froze. Processing with her mind, she thought of her parents, her aunt and her little sister Magda. She was not ready to grow up. She had few other options. This duplicitous Sargent made himself sound so generous. Lily was growing old enough to know the difference.

You are Rest and Peace

"My aunt processed what I told her pretty calmly. She seemed so strong. She knew better. She gave off this air of normalcy and equanimity. She didn't panic. She remained calm. More calm than me, I couldn't sleep. I struggled to think about how we would tell mama and papa. This went on for days. Finally, Nicola took it all on herself. She said simply, 'I will tell them'. I was so relieved not to tell my parents. I don't know why. I was ashamed. Not of being Jewish, I was ashamed to be so scared."

"You were just 14. Don't you think it's a bit unrealistic to think you would not be scared?", Jennifer's posed as a simple reminder.

As Lily nodded, the tears started again. "They had no right...no right to make me hide so much...to make me lie."

"Our singing began that next day. My aunt and I simply walked into the patisserie. Our smile gave away our acceptance of their bargain.

Our singing seemed to genuinely lift these two officious Germans. Awkward to say the least, we would arrive mid-afternoon as the Captain received his afternoon tea. He'd been educated for two years of college at Oxford in England. Our songs seemed familiar to both of these Hun officers. I cannot say they grew on us. We never loss that unease as we entered the Captain's office. Still, we developed a routine as the summer sun lowered itself into autumn.

My aunt Nicola became my compass in this foreign territory. She helped me form a strong carriage and backbone. Whenever the officers invited us to linger or stay, she would gently and firmly say it was time for us to leave. On occasion, the officers would be busy with an exercise or drill. When the Captain's steward would let us know the officers were away, I was relieved. While the anxiety of these afternoon recitals made me feel quite alive, they would drain away my energy as we finished. They weighed even more heavily on my conscience."

Again Jennifer would pull Lily away from assessments and ask her how she felt as she sang, drank tea and interacted with the officers. "What would they say? How did they look at you? Can you describe the room, the cookies, the tea?"

Lily swallowed hard as she began.

"The Captain would look condescendingly. Oxford did not soften his envy and contempt for the riches and lavish homes of those Jewish merchants in his native Berlin. He couldn't reconcile his attraction with his contempt for our obvious Semitism. The young Sargent smiled unconsciously, almost thoughtlessly. My aunt worried that the Captain had become infatuated with me. I was too young to make those distinctions. I didn't like his look or how he looked at me. It was too close to staring. Polite but his gaze lingered too long, as he was taking me into his eyes. Nicola observed all of it and enforced a start and finish that left little room for improprieties."

Jennifer asked firmly, "had he fallen in love with you?"

"At the time, I couldn't say. He seemed coarse and predatory in his gaze. I didn't know what love looked like. Thinking back, no, I suspect he just wanted my developing adolescent body. I shudder at the image, even the idea of it.

He seemed hollow, dull and a bit removed from the power he and the Sargent possessed. Still, the Sargent would follow his orders. For that, there was no doubt. You could tell from his obsequious, fawning manner that the Sargent wouldn't challenge his superior. They were everyday Germans with a very blurred sense of right and wrong. Like others, they allowed themselves to be complicit, a couple more useful cogs in this growing madness."

Singing *"You are Rest and Peace"* seemed so sinister and incongruous. No rest or peace came from this singing, not for me, my aunt or even these robotic Germans. Around us in Leopoldstadt, rest and peace became more scarce every day of that late autumn of 1938. More and more families disappeared. Some escaped quietly and secretly. Some were taken away by the Germans. 'Going north' or 'east' meant only concentration camps. Prominentes might be taken to Mauthausen which meant Austria. Most went north to Dachau or Buchenwald.

Because so many of the Jews in our section of Vienna performed as musicians, or attained recognition as artists and scholars, Dachau and Mauthausen became the camps we heard about the most. Dachau became known as a Civil Internment Camp. Jews deemed to possess "exchange value" were kept in these camps. Their crematorium facilities were smaller and hidden out of sight. Starvation and disease replaced gassing and cremation. A different kind of Rest and Peace prevailed, one formed from a mindless brutality, one German sycophant at a time.

They Just Disappeared

"Singing at tea time almost became routine."

"Almost", she swallowed very slowly and hard.

"Autumn slipped into the winter and the holidays of Hanukkah and Christmas. We sang for the officers many of their holiday songs, *My Tannenbaum* and *Silent Night*. It became a bit routine and yet their songs reminded my aunt and me at the harsh reality lurking just under the placid look of these two Germans. Obsessing about their repulsive Jews while trying to pay us the compliment of staring at our feminine figures.

During this time period, talk began among the Jews of these "concentration camps". The names we heard most frequently Dachau, Buchenwald and, of course, Mauthausen. As often as we heard their mention, my father would continue to believe his "privileged" status would protect him and us. His good friend Meyer as a lawyer insisted he knew all the particulars of the Nuremberg Laws. He kept saying that prominent Jews whose grandparents were not both Jewish would be safe. These laws were so crazy. Can you imagine government ministers in suits and ties writing such laws? Deciding how Jewish you were by how many of your grandparents were Jewish... this contempt flowed from that envy. It began as coarse class warfare. As our two German voyeurs mixed that with religion, yellow stars, and the Yid taunts and slogans, it made for a poisonous stew...a stew they seem to like the taste.

"We were so naive...so naive."

The young German Sargent had grown up in Heidelberg and hoped for a career in the German Navy. However, during the trials for the nautical college at Bremerhaven, he flunked the swimming test. His mother taught him to read music and he hoped to study the piano and harpsichord. Yet, he knew the circumstances of his birth. As the son of a guilder, university remained an elusive far-off idea. He knew of wealthy piano students whose families could finance such studies. Jewish merchants and bankers could afford these kinds of indulgences for their children. Despite his mother's encouragement, for him, it was not to be. He carried this resentment in hidden baggage below the surface. It came when he needed a target to off load his bitterness. Lily's parents proved useful. His confusion between attraction and envy for Lily kept him muted in his expressions. Conflict raged inside him. Rage that needed a mark. It all wound itself into a ball of confused emotional string.

Part of this young Sargent struggled with the persecution of the Jews. Once a young music student, this young Lily Mendelssohn seemed not that far from his own struggle. Her parents' and their plight caused him little concern. This young girl singing so beautifully seemed much like how he thought of himself. He thought that these tea time singings might just take her out of her home when the SS arrived. However confused the motives of the young Sargent, the Captain carried darker obsessions.

The odious Captain found the time away from his family and wife difficult to endure. He said as much to both Nicola and Lily.

"I could tell that the officers began to cling to us too much. They alluded to how lonely it could be serving in the Army so far from home. As my aunt processed all of this lurking behavior, she announced one day to me very simply: 'Our time in Austria cannot last much longer. Your father must face the reality. We must leave.'

I had become vaguely aware of her budding friendship with Anton Rabinowitz whom she'd meet at synagogue. She assured me that, at some point, we might need his help. His work with Jewish refugees would only be discussed in the most hushed tones. My aunt was a realist. She was also very shrewd."

"A month after Passover in the spring of '39, it happened. As we walked back down the dark stairway from the Captain's office, we heard the distinctive siren of the unmarked SS cars. They were just leaving down the main boulevard of Leopoldstadt. As we approached our building, the owner of the patisserie just stared at us with the most mournful eyes. While we'd been down the block, upstairs singing, the SS entered our home. They probably took what they wanted. The owner's look gave everything away. The SS simply took away my parents and Magda. Just like that, they were gone…just disappeared."

Numb from Head to Toe

Jennifer inched closer to Lily as she asked, "at that moment standing at the entrance of the patisserie, how would you describe it?"

"I just froze.

I became numb.

It was as if my toes and fingers tingled and couldn't move.

Slow motion, everything slowed to a halt."

As her words failed her, her eyes widened. Her fingers stretched out long and tight. Jennifer could feel Lily look right through her.

"They were gone." As her eyes widened even further.

"They were gone."

"Mother standing in our kitchen. Reminding me to finish my soup"

"My father sitting at the table in the bay window. With the morning's *Neues Wiener Tagblatt* opened in his outstretched hands, smiling at me, his darling Lily."

"Magda with her nose buried, reading her books."

"When did this numb feeling begin?" as Jennifer gently and firmly helped Lily trace her feelings.

Lily swallowed hard and very slowly.

"I guess long before that day...I think I became numb the day we started singing. Everyday walking with my aunt to the Captain's office. Everyday the silence surrounding my family. The secrecy, the hiding of it all. These officers imaging their way with me. The fear, numb to everything....all the time."

Gentle slow tears draped Lily's cheeks. This cognition came slowly. Numb became her default state. Far too real and painful was the loss of parents, a sister, her grandmother and the circumstances that led to it. Numb became her anesthetic. Her way of coping.

This cognition brought relief. It lightened her.

"It was my aunt Nicola who kept her wits about her. She tugged firmly on my light coat and said, 'Come Lily, we must go. We must not go home.' She was so right. Walking into our building would have meant the same fate for us. The Nazis were probably picking through our family belongings even then. Nicola guided me across the broad avenue, and across the park to the street car line. With its power rod crackling above, it slowed to pick up some passengers. We hurried and made it onto the street car. Instincts told me where we were going. Across the river brucke, a circuitous route to throw off anyone following us. Eventually, we made it into the Neubaugurtel. Anton Rabinowitz knew where to hide. Even shrewder than Nicola, he knew that Vienna's Red Light district made the perfect hiding place for a Jew and an occasional Nazi corpse."

Uncle Anton

"Anton Rabinowitz opened the door to his small flat above a particularly pungent Viennese burlesque parlor. I'd never been to the Neubaugurtel. My eyes could hardly take in all of what passed as city life under his flat. These half-naked women were actually standing, sitting and posing in the bay windows of these brothels. At fifteen, this all was very new to me. Some of these women seemed my age. We were a long way from our family playing music and singing in our respectable Viennese townhouse. Although only fifteen, I could tell from the embrace Aunt Nicola gave Anton that they were not merely friends. This was not the first time Nicola had been to Anton's flat. As I looked over the documents and photographs strewn across his oversized desk, I peeked at my aunt deeply into Anton's arms.

The scope of his refugee work came into focus. He was literally moving hundreds of Jews out of Vienna, out of Austria and out of Europe. Used train tickets laying on his desk included cities like Amsterdam, Siena, and Marseilles. Part savior, part sneaky bastard, my respect for him grew as I sized up the scale of his work."

"How did he seem to you? How did he and Nicola seem together? asked Jennifer.

"Being fifteen, I was probably unsure. But, I think I thought there were lovers."

Jennifer shook her head and couldn't hide her curiousness, "how did you ever escape?"

"Well, my aunt couldn't hide things much longer..."

"Hide what?" Jennifer insisted.

"She and Anton had secretly eloped. This elopement carried only one condition on the part of my aunt. She insisted that they would leave Austria and live in America. Nicola worked it out in her mind. The three of us would, if necessary, escape...together."

"But your parents?" Jennifer couldn't help but wonder.

"I think Nicola had given up on convincing them. She loved them, but she thought them too patient and Olympian in their willingness to endure the Nazis and their chipping away at our way of life. These new laws made it difficult for Jews to own businesses and property. The Nazis concocted Byzantine layers of rules and regulations. My aunt saw past all of that nonsense. She knew the rules would forever be made into higher and higher hurdles. My parents followed rules. Nicola knew better. Nicola saw the irrationality of the rules and the sinister motives behind the rule making. Her cunning mind could think for itself. Even more than Anton, she could see the larger picture. In Hebrew, she would say, "lech le ha". It means simply "get out".

"Your parents?" once again asked Jennifer.

"Bergen Belsen, the word came through the underground and the synagogues. Most of the Viennese Jews were sent to Bergen Belsen. Described as a 'Residence Camp', it housed many of the artists and musicians. The SS thought exchanges could be arranged for spies and Germans in other countries. Crazy! Who would want to come to Germany. You'd have to be nuts! Even if you were German! No one would volunteer for such an exchange.

Anton worked out the documents. Forged and of very high quality, Anton and Nicola became my parents, my adopted parents. In reality, he became Uncle Anton."

Refugee Musicians Committee

"We wasted very little time. Anton knew the Germans would figure out that some of the musical Mendelssohn family evaded capture." Jennifer finally settled into what had transpired.

"So, in reality you didn't abandon or give up your parents. You see the role your aunt played? Right?" Jennifer's voice firmed as she posed the question.

"I chose to sing. They had asked me. I included Nicola. But, they asked me."

"Did you think that your singing would save all of your family?" Jennifer posited.

"Oh, I was so naive. It was pathetic how innocent I was! Of course, I thought I could protect all of my family. So stupid…".

As Lily caught her breath, her tears began anew as she chuckled.

"What was I thinking! Did I really think…as a fifteen year old girl that I could save us? I guess it was a teenager seeing herself in a grand role…"

"Pretty unrealistic…" Jennifer helped her catch her breath.

"Where did the three of you go? How did Anton know what to do next?" Jennifer demurred, taking her memory to its next file.

"I learned pretty quickly that Nicola and Anton had been planning our escape for some time. They forged documents, the old family photos planted as evidence, their wedding bands and our family jewelry as barter, they'd thought of so many details. I was just catching up…"

"Anton explained to me all about the various groups helping Jews to escape Germany, the Sudetenland and

Austria. He said that soon they would be organized under the 'Jewish Refugee Service'. As this new group's primary contact in Vienna, his effort focused on musicians and performers. Honoring his marriage vow to my aunt meant he'd been actively looking for an enterprising Viennese Jew to take over his work. This subgroup called itself the 'Musicians Emergency Fund'. Bernhard Edelman worked as a young banking associate at Raiffeisen Bank. Anton used to joke that Bernie knew where the money was…he helped raise the funds for their refugee work. Bernie looked so mature, so much older. Every once and awhile, I would catch myself staring at him. He was so handsome…and smart. But, he was older. It went on for months, yet he was always proper. But, even then we both knewv"

"Knew what?" Jennifer asked plainly.

"Once we all arrived in Chicago, I married Bernhard Edelman. He was my husband. We waited until I was eighteen. He helped me with my English, my schooling. He was the finest man I've ever known. In those early days, he was above reproach. He said later, 'you made me want to be a better man'. I could not have been more fortunate. I was the first refugee musician that he helped to escape."

Casino Estoril

How did you get to Chicago? Jennifer began with amazement.

"Via Portugal, we used to joke that Estoril was Nicola and Anton's honeymoon. Prior to leaving Austria for Portugal, Bernie told us that his eldest brother Erwin had moved from Vienna to Chicago in late 1928 to work at the Foreman Bank. Erwin worked closely with Walter Head as they merged the State Bank into the Foreman. As one of the largest banks in Chicago, the Foreman State included many of Chicago's wealthiest Jewish families as its clients. Bernie arranged in advance for Anton to work at the Foreman assisting with its banking for clients moving their businesses to America. Bernie could see the role Chicago would have as the banking center for the American middle west. The Crash had hit Midwest merchant banks hard and Chicago began to emerge as the dominant banking center west of New York. I actually think, even then, that Bernie envisioned us together in Chicago."

"Why Portugal?" Jennifer wanted to make sure not to miss any of the details of the escape and those difficult travel episodes.

"Lisbon with its large natural harbor on the Atlantic Ocean became a transshipment point for refugees. This ship "EE Belle" became our way out of Europe. Bernie's brother Erwin seemed to have worked out the details. How? I'm not exactly sure. These documents Anton had created in Vienna seem to be the key."

"How did you afford this trip? That ship captain must have extorted very high fares, particularly for three Jews trying to leave for America?"

"Oh, he did. But my aunt could be very crafty. We met this roguish ship captain in the casino in Estoril. This casino became a sort of currency exchange for human trafficking. Most nights, desperate refugees would try to bargain an escape. We were just three more…

Nicola and Anton brought me along as they made the first in a series of "payments".

"Payments? What kind of payments?" Jennifer could not hid her curiousness.

"Aunt Nicola had agreed to keep our family diamonds safe for my grandmother. They were emerald and brilliant cuts and of great clarity and color. The ship captain could hardly control himself. Anton let the captain know this small brilliant cut was merely a "deposit". Once we arrived safely on board in our own room, another "deposit". Once we were safely underway to America, another diamond would be given to him. Once we arrived in America and passed through customs, a final and most valuable stone would be turned over to him. The captain couldn't figure out where my uncle and aunt hid these diamonds. But, he couldn't resist. Our escape and ship passage became almost comfortable. Compared to the cramp quarters of the other refugees, our cabin was actually spacious and humane. My aunt and uncle saved me.

"Indeed! This is a remarkable story. At fifteen, you helped them pull it off." Jennifer offered.

"We celebrated my sixteenth birthday in that casino. My aunt bought me a champagne cocktail as my birthday present."

"A cold cocktail, only seems right. Such a chilling tale…". Jennifer grimaced.

Chicago…First back to Vienna

"How did your aunt and uncle keep the diamonds safe and hidden?" Jennifer inquired.

"Let's just say my aunt's skills as a seamstress and her elegant posture came in ample supply."

"Keeping things hidden may have been my family's greatest strength."

"And weakness?" Jennifer offered.

"It was here in Lisbon with just a few hours to go before our departure, that I hazarded a long letter to my parents. We thought we could mail it just before our departure, and then we couldn't be traced and tracked. I sat in our cabin on the ship and wrote draft after draft but struggled to form the words. My silent bargain with that German Sargent began to weigh more and more heavily and profoundly on my conscience. The Sargent said to me, 'the Captain will make it safe for you…and your aunt'."

"How could I do it!!!!" Lily screamed.

Lily's shriek shook Jennifer to the core. Jennifer could see Lily's shoulders and head slump as the weight she was carrying began to lighten. As the energy and light drained out of Lily, her counselor sensed the intensity of this deeply charged memory rising to the surface. Lily looked right through Jennifer as she begged "how could I abandon my parents? Magda? My grandmother? How! How!! How!!!…"

"At fourteen, who were you not to stand up to the full force, might and depravity of the Third Reich?" Jennifer took the plunge and chanced framing the enormity of Lily's unrealistic expectation of herself.

Lily just stared the blankest of stares.

Then, Jennifer raised the stakes even further on Lily. "Do you really prefer martyrdom?"

Lily just looked right through her trusted confidante. Opening her moist eyes wide as she began to fully process the illusion she'd put on herself these last forty years. Her mask began to slip and fall away and she couldn't help herself...as she chuckled at her own self-deception. Her own private con game that she'd perpetrated on herself. The illusion of her failing to accept her own fourteen year old flawed humaneness. A fifty-eight year old women letting go of lofty expectations she'd put on herself as a frightened young Jewish teenager in Nazi controlled Austria. She began slowly to awaken and see herself evenly and more rationally.

Lily came to understand that from this loss, she brought a deep guilt. Laying on herself unrealistic expectations, she buried her loss inside martyrdom and shame. Letting herself off the hook lightened her load, and her anger.

She would have written a very different letter to her parents after her mind bending cognition. A very different letter, a letter she never had a chance to write.

She said weeping and simply, "that afternoon with the evening tide, my aunt and I, with uncle Anton as our protector, set sail for a New World. We began a different life I could not have imagined only twelve months earlier. America means different things to different people. To the three of us as immigrants, it meant a new life. With Bernhard's arrival late the following year, a new start. A new beginning—that allowed us to move past the choices we'd made and all the loss we carried. If only a person could be apportioned two lives, a life to live and a life to use to learn how to live. That's what America and Chicago would mean for the four of us - our family."

Observing Lily Edelman changed me. Coming to know her story gave meaning and depth to the Hebrew holidays and traditions I only heard about and knew superficially as a boy. Stoic and proud, she became softer and more rounded in front of our eyes. Her pain came from the deepest basement of time —a place few of us can remotely imagine. She showed such great courage as a young Austrian Jew. She demonstrated an even greater courage at nearly sixty years of age. She made a path for herself that we rarely see. She chose her new life. Her best version of herself became her most courageous choice.

Friday was the day for our final presentations. That Friday afternoon, just after we finished lunch, Lily sang to us our last presentation of the week. "Edelweiss" as an Austrian lullaby moistened our eyes. Absent the anger and edge of bitterness, she once again had us spellbound. Seeing through to her essential self, an angel came alive through that voice. We couldn't resist being moved. She had us, mind ~ body ~ spirit. Each note took you to a higher and higher plain. Her voice reclaimed everyone.

31

Mayor Jane Jacobs

L earning the ropes at Balcor took nine years. Learning the ropes of the investment business took almost as long. Learning the ropes at Wall Street also took too long. My ethical compass began to spin. Wall Street seemed way better at manufacturing investments than being entrusted with other people's money. Finally, I left and settled on returning to Ann Arbor for graduate school.

The masters program in Urban and Regional Planning became my new "job." Inevitably, the program fully exposed me to the urban catastrophe known as "Detroit." From the failures of Wall Street to do what's right. I studied first hand political leaders not doing what's right.

As far back as Augustus B. Woodward, Detroit has been subject to the grandiose visions of self-obsessed political leaders. Described as a prototype for Ichabod Crane, Augustus Woodward was appointed Chief Justice of the Michigan Territory immediately following the great fire that swept Detroit in June of 1805. Ambitious—he was nominated by none other than Thomas Jefferson—and known for his habitual slovenliness, Woodward laid out the radial streets that came to distinguish Detroit. Woodward also provided the vision for the University of Michigan, which opened its doors— originally in Detroit—in 1817.

Fast forward to the next great crisis. The Great Depression of the 1930s led the Burroughs Corporation to "loan" Albert Cobo, one of its finance executives, to assist the city of Detroit. Known mainly for his determined effort to remove the city's streetcars, Mayor Cobo also oversaw the demolition of the two city neighborhoods dominated by African Americans—Black Bottom and Paradise Valley. The drive to eliminate these unsightly but stable neighborhoods led Cobo and his successor, Louis Marini, to bulldoze a total of sixty square blocks into what became known as "Ragweed Acres"—no builders showed interest in redevelopment. Not to be deterred from their goal of urban renewal and "helping the poor," the city—with federal assistance—subsidized the construction of multiple stand-alone high rise apartments. This new neighborhood fared no better than its predecessor. You might wonder why the idea that something else might be wrong never took root…

As these large-scale planning efforts began to take shape—and fail—in Detroit, a young urban activist named Jane Jacobs began to articulate an alternative view of how to save cities and promote their good health. Originally, Jacobs helped organize the opposition to the construction of the Lower Manhattan Expressway, which would have bisected SoHo and Little Italy in New York City. Profoundly simple in her approach, Jacobs viewed poverty in a fundamentally different light.

"To seek 'causes' of poverty in this way is to enter an intellectual dead end," she stated, "because poverty has no causes. Only 'prosperity' has causes."

Poverty is the default state of the human species. Prosperity results from organizing human activity.

Jacobs represented a full rejection of the zero sum mentality of urban planning. Rather than figure out how to house, accommodate, and segregate the poor and middle class, she viewed their presence as one of many real keys to genuine urban health. She saw encouraging mixing between people who did not know each other—a density of strangers who could cogitate new activities, businesses, and enterprises—as a simple solution that could revitalize a city. In her view, density was to be encouraged; it provided a key to the unexpected and unplanned ways cities could grow and evolve. Cities should not mimic the suburbs. They could and should be fundamentally different.

Detroiters know very well that the ideas of Jane Jacobs didn't get the time of day. Instead, Mayor Jerry Cavanaugh doubled down on the grand planning schemes of his Republican predecessors, joining with President Lyndon Johnson to establish "Model Cities," a city income tax, and a commuter tax as ways to "save" Detroit. By the time Mayor Coleman Young arrived, the harebrained schemes had reached their zenith in the national disgrace of the Detroit "People Mover," a rail oddity that became a cruel metaphor for the flight of taxpayers and businesses from the low density wasteland Detroit's planners had created.

Let's consider for a minute what might have happened had Detroit elected Jane Jacobs as Mayor beginning in the 1950s:

- Forget the freeways; keep the streetcars
- Rebuild the neighborhoods with lending; don't raze them
- More magnet and charter schools, not fewer
- No housing projects, loans to small businesses instead
- Let neighbors help provide active surveillance instead of more police
- Let Vegas keep the casinos
- Tax consumption, not growth and incomes
- Invest in people, not buildings or projects

As Jacobs said, "The trouble with paternalists is that they want to make impossibly profound changes, and they choose impossibly superficial means for doing so."

What would be different? Let's count the ways. Instead of displacing large numbers of poor by government fiat, a slower, more organic process would and should have occurred. Eliminate the byzantine crazyquilt of city planning, density, and building restrictions. Let property owners decide for themselves. If the residents of Black Bottom and Paradise Valley really were situated too close to downtown, they would have benefitted as development *sought those parcels so close to the city center.* The key rests with allowing stakeholders the latitude and freedom to experiment and learn from trial and error *on a small scale.*

So, if small is beautiful, how small do we go? Or, to be more precise, *how* do we go small?

- Districts should include at least two different property uses—preferably more.
- Streets should be short, not more than a few blocks.
- Streets should be narrower, thus slowing traffic.
- Arterial roadways should be well landscaped, with ample buffers.
- Small pocket parks, and open areas on rivers and lakes, should be encouraged.
- Sports stadiums and megamuseums should not be subsidized.
- Simplify licensing requirements for small businesses and street vendors.
- Special requirements for multi-use property owners should be eliminated.

Detroit practiced largescale planning with public and private funds on such a scale that the word *Detroit* at one time, became synonymous with urban failure in America. It's understandable—when a community manufactures military vehicles so prodigiously that Nazi Germany puts it near the top of its bombing target list, we cannot blame our leaders for thinking everything should be done bigger and better. Unfortunately, facilitating the health of a city differs radically from defeating totalitarianism and tyranny. More nurture and nature will serve Detroit better as we emerge from this latest crisis of municipal bankruptcy and reorganization. This time, let's take it slow and small. Build Detroit from the bottom up, not from the top down. An important lesson about human problem solving that would be re-affirmed in the next phase of my career.

32

Zen Capital

Eight months of interviewing finally landed me the offer. I accepted. It's as if the long interview process itself served to sell me on the company. I would be "carrying the bag," representing American Funds' Capital Research and Management in Michigan. Known to its associates and clients as Capital, it might be more accurate to describe it during those heady years as Zen Capital, one of the most enigmatic, nuanced, and successful companies in American business history—a company worth studying. Here is some of what I learned there.

Sales

Nothing happens in a business until the client opens up the checkbook or says to the salesperson, "Let's buy it." In the American mutual fund industry, buying funds remained the domain of stockbrokers and financial planners until the early 1970s. With the advent of tollfree telephone calling, two fund companies, Fidelity and Vanguard, emerged to enable the direct purchase of mutual fund shares. Fidelity became a behemoth in the American fund industry by removing their advisers as the broker of record. They went on to grow from the base of assets those advisers had brought them. Vanguard went direct on day one. This could have been the demise of broker sold funds. For American Funds, it was like Christmas Day. From then on, American Funds would be the company that never screwed the broker—not a bad brand on which to build.

American Funds and its Zenlike parent, Capital, went on to become the company to provide what advisers and their clients genuinely needed. There was a huge distinction right there—the clients belonged to the adviser. American Funds would view the adviser as the client. Capital would manage the fund for the benefit of the shareholder; however, American Funds Distributors (AFD) would focus on the adviser as the client. It may not seem like a big deal to the casual observer, but that distinction made all the difference and really separated AFD from the competition.

Pricing

The change from front end load only to a combination of frontend with a trailing service fee came about in 1988, to keep the relationship between the adviser and client close and robust throughout the period of ownership of the fund shares. The market crash in October of 1987 brought that imperative front and center.

Objections to the front end load came in daily. Our response was always a variation of the adage, "the least cost is the lowest cost when it's the last cost." Pay it once as a smaller percentage of your capital, and don't pay again—pretty simple. Still, our wholesalers dealt with this objection to the front end load constantly. One day I took a call from a Merrill Lynch manager in the Deep South. "Kirk, we've got a problem again. Joe's calling the brokers 'wussies' for not being man enough to sell the A share (front end load)." Time for another session with Human Resources for old Joe. But you had to admire his guts. He was right on the mark.

If a prospective shareholder contacted us directly to acquire a fund, that would be another variation on the pricing issue. Our response remained consistent; they would be asked simply, "Who is your adviser?" Eventually, the no load buyer would either pound his head in frustration or go find an adviser. Sure enough, we would either have a new adviser to potentially treat as a client, or we would have reinforced, for an existing adviser, that we meant what we said: the adviser was the client. It probably seems "pollyannish" to think about a company being so clear and centered on such simple concepts. Yet, back in the kitchen and behind the scenes, it always seemed to hang together.

Investment Results

Nowhere did our attention to the needs of advisers make itself more known than in Capital's management of fund assets. Eschewing both the "star" manager system and the committee structure, Capital created teams of portfolio counselors and analysts, each managing a "sleeve" or a portion of the fund. The benefits of this system over time became legendary and manifold:

- No manager or counselor became indispensable to the fund.
- Retirements and departures could be handled without disruption and fanfare.
- Managers and analysts would share ideas but make their own decisions.
- Owning only their highest conviction ideas meant the funds would include no "filler."
- As funds grew or shrank, counselors could be added or dropped easily.
- Fund results (never referred to as "performance") tended to be smoother and less volatile as investments achieved diversification without mimicking indexes.
- Investment results beat the indexes during "down" periods when advisers most needed superior results.

- Advisers found that they were most vulnerable to losing clients during market downturns, not because their portfolios lagged hot markets during strong upswings.
- "Lonely" and novel investment ideas could be owned and, as conviction spread, these concentrations could become large and meaningful. Examples included AOL, Chrysler, and Apple.

Sales Stories

Detroit stockbrokers used to recount story after story of American Funds' sales meetings, shareholders' reallife experiences, and mythical sales pitches that illustrated different sales ideas that would help clients be patient, thoughtful, and ultimately more successful. A few stand out as most colorful and compelling:

"Afternoon Tea"

In the early days before plane flight became affordable and common, AFD's wholesalers would travel the country by train. One of the more colorful early sales guys was Ward Bishop. He traveled most of the large eastern cities like Pittsburgh, Washington, D.C., and the original home of Jonathan B. Lovelace, Detroit.

Jonathan Bell Lovelace served as an artillery officer during World War I. Serving with the son of E.C. MacCrone, he gained notoriety for his facile use of trigonometry in targeting artillery strikes. At the end of the war, young MacCrone convinced his father of Lovelace's prodigious math skills, and they recruited him to their Detroit-based firm.

Starting as a statistician for MacCrone and Company, Mr. Lovelace brought to his Mac-Crone partners the original idea for a Master Trust or mutual fund. Closedend (which simply meant it traded like a stock) and leveraged, these trusts became very popular in the Roaring Twenties. Lovelace helped pioneer this concept for MacCrone and Company, but he encouraged them to rein in their fund beginning in early 1928.

He knew valuations well enough to understand the risk that was building in the stock market as stock ownership spread to masses of Americans. Unable to convince his partners to be more prudent, he asked to be bought out—a request they accommodated in late 1928.

Moving to Southern California, Lovelace set up shop as Capital Research in Los Angeles. After the crash, the Trust lost over 90 percent of its value, wiping out MacCrone and Company and landing the original fund in bankruptcy court. The bankruptcy judge, looking for ways to reorganize the fund, sought out Lovelace in California as someone who might be able to assist with the workout. His idea was fairly straightforward: shareholders would be allowed to trade their shares for warrants (a right to buy a security at an agreed price) in a new fund. That new fund came to be known as the Investment Company of America (ICA), the flagship of the American Funds family.

By the 1950s, the fund's assets had grown to over half a billion dollars. Ward Bishop became its finest spokesperson, often presiding over "afternoon tea." Mastering the art of droll, tongue-in-cheek communication, Ward simply secured the largest ballroom at the finest hotel in Detroit, the Book Cadillac, and stocked a bar with a groaning supply of hard spirits. Once he finished his short talk on ICA, the drapery would be pulled back and stockbrokers from all over Motown would unwind, relax, and ultimately need to take a street car back to hearth and home.

Boones and Clausens

One of the more puzzling aspects of selling a mutual fund is the standardized language: "Past returns are no guarantee of future results." Pick up a prospectus, and that language will appear early and often. Nothing demonstrated the axiom more effectively than the simple story of the Boones and the Clausens.

These two mythic couples simply made two different types of investments, and their results told you everything you needed to know. The Boones suffered from a stale marriage. Dour and unpleasant in the extreme, they bought fixed income. The poor Boones, fixed for the rest of their lives, could not keep up with inflation—or the Clausens.

Mr. and Mrs. Clausen put their savings into ICA and took a portion, usually around five to six percent, as income for the rest of their lives. Driving in a nice Cadillac with big smiles on their faces, the Clausens lived better than the Boones. Although the Clausens lived with the risk of their nest egg fluctuating in value year to year as markets climbed up and down, their nest egg continued to grow, as did the income they could draw from it. One of our more enterprising wholesalers actually cut out a picture of Mrs. Boone and placed her in the back seat of the Clausens' convertible, leaving poor Mr. Boone to be dour and riskaverse all by himself.

My "Ike-A"

Early in my American Funds career as the sales person in Michigan, the Swiss company Sandoz bought Gerber, the baby food company headquartered in Greenville, Michigan. Puréed carrots, peas and beans made for big business. Included among these overnight Gerber millionaires would be the many local farmers who during leaner years accepted scrip instead of full cash payment. An enterprising investment representative with Edward D. Jones took full advantage by helping these Gerber shareholders manage their stock sales and redeploy their proceeds prudently into broadly diversified baskets of blue chip securities.

This local Jones investment representative (IR) called me soon after the acquisition. Through his office, a large number of shareholders in our funds suddenly found themselves able to make substantial additional investments. The Jones IR wanted to schedule a shareholder meeting sooner rather than later. Of course, I agreed. He caught me a little off guard when he told me the location of the meeting would be the "Sugar Shack" in nearby Juggville, Michigan.

Legendary for high quality cakes and fruit pies made from locally sourced fruit harvested by nearby cherry and peach farmers, the "Sugar Shack" provided the perfect lure and bait to ensure a full house for this American Funds shareholders meeting. Indeed, by the time I'd arrived and set up my slide projector and annual reports, everyone found a piece of pie to their liking and cold iced tea or hot coffee. The prepared shareholder meeting content lasted about 35 minutes. The Q & A that followed always distinguished the best meetings from the so-so gatherings. This night stood out from most.

As the Q & A began to wind down, an very stooped and well-dressed elderly lady stood up, raised her hand, and asked if she "could make a few comments about my Ike-A (ICA or Investment Company of America)?".

Glancing at the Edward Jones man, I can see him nodding furiously in the affirmative.

"Sure, please share your thoughts with us…"

She began tentatively,

"Well…when my late husband Henry was about to finish his service as radioman on the USS Enterprise in World War II, he begun to write in his letters about us getting married. My father was adamant that there'd be no talk of a wedding unless Henry "could show savings". So, Henry accepted his Navy pay and after buying a train ticket back to Michigan and buying a new suit, he bought some Ike-A (ICA or Investment Company of America) with his leftover pay."

The Edward Jones man later filled in the details. Henry and Beulah Heidbreder brought to their young marriage a keen eye for saving money and stretching a dollar. Rather than pay an electrician for repairs, Henry kept up his skills as a radioman. Beulah took canning of fruits and vegetables a bit further than her fellow Greenville wives. Sweet gherkins became a family favorite passed down to her daughters and grand daughters. Plane travel seemed expensive and paled in remembrances when compared with family road trips to Benzie County. Climbing sand dunes, fishing the Betsey and canoeing and camping along side the Platte River filled their family memory bank. Money saved could be added to their ICA. This "Greatest Generation" really did earn their greatness and saved it for later.

Beulah continued. "Henry always said, 'we could use the dividends if we need them, but that we should never touch the capital'. So, he and I stuck by that rule. After he passed, the taxes owed on these dividends and reinvested gains started to be harder and harder to pay. Then, our Edward Jones man sat with me and explained it's, in fact, okay to use some of the reinvested gains to pay the taxes. So, I've been doing just that for the last ten years. Then, I learned that if I give some of my gains to our church, that would really reduce my taxes. So, those of you that attend church with me. You know that's how I could help fund that new chapel at Holy Child."

"So, I've been able to help my kids with their houses, and my church, and there's still enough left over that I think Henry would be pleased…I like my Ike-A". It's been wonderful for us."

So the sooner I shut up the better, I wished I could have taken that sweet old lady to all my shareholder meetings. Her story from Greenville became worth its weight in gold.

Louie the Loser

By far the most iconic figure in the American mutual fund industry, Louie portrayed investors' biggest fear and turned it to his advantage. For many of us, investing remains a test of our ability to resist the extremes of fear and greed that plague us when it comes time to invest our sacred nest egg. My mentor said once, "Only three things motivate people: fear, sex and greed. The investment business will never be sexy, so we're left with fear and greed."

Most investors fear at a base level that the day they choose to invest will be the wrong day. Left to look at their investment the next day or the day after, they fear that it will drop, or drop again. The simple story of Louie the Loser stares down this basic fear. Louie only invests on the worst possible day. For twenty straight years, he invests on the market high for the year. Forget the fact that statistically, it's virtually impossible to be that unlucky; Louie is that unlucky—and he's laughing all the way to the bank. The five thousand dollars he's invested every year—for a total of one hundred thousand—have grown to two or three times that amount, proving that it's **time in** the market, not **timing** of the market. Louie became almost as big as our American Funds brand. Virtually every stockbroker in America knew or used Louie. He was that big.

Marketing

Most salespeople spend their Monday mornings throwing (or now recycling) marketing materials into the dumpster. Wow! At AFD, we actually used the stuff. What a concept—marketing material that sales people used every day. Creating new marketing material at AFD was a triennial process—underline the word "process."

Three times a year, the leadership of AFD would convene a small group of marketing staff, two wholesalers, a relationship manager, and one of the division managers who oversaw a region of wholesalers. This group would lock themselves away for a day and a half and undergo a story-development process. This story would then be presented to the sales force at the upcoming triennial national sales meeting. Discipline characterized the process, but it allowed for creativity at the same time. It's how the secret sauce was prepared.

Coached by the Fusion Group of Weston, Florida, this process became synonymous with the high quality of American Funds' marketing materials and our very disciplined presentation style. Formal but free flowing, colorful and compelling, short and sweet; AFD used this fusion process and the resulting materials to build its reputation as the best marketers in the fund industry.

Armature under a piece of artistic sculpture provides a form and skeleton that the sculptor uses as a base or starting point. The process taught to us by the Fusion Group and its trainers served as an armature for our triennial campaigns. You could almost describe the process as reverse engineering of persuasive communication:

Begin With the End in Mind

We started at the end by asking ourselves what exactly we wanted the listener to do as a concrete action step. When? Where? And sometimes, how? It might be as simple as, "Go to your iPad this afternoon, access our website, and download the newest 'Louie the Loser' illustration." We kept it clear, explicit, and simple.

Why and Why Not?

The longest part of the process for the campaign development team would be to ask itself why the listener would or would not take our explicit action step. The roots of this brand of persuasion can be traced to Aristotle, who created the framework of "pro/con" rhetoric. If we can clearly identify why an audience might not do what we ask, we can then transcend that resistance and move them to action.

"Too busy with other stuff," "I already know Louie," "The investment landscape is different this time." With the objections clearly identified, we would provide a compelling and tailored response to every objection and form of resistance. "Let the website do the work for you," "This Louie illustration reflects today's global environment." "History may not repeat itself, but it rhymes." Typically, a main idea that we could use as a launch for the next step we wanted the prospect to take would emerge.

Organize Your Key Points

Once we had organized our pros and cons, we would separate them into three or four descriptors. It might be as simple as "problem," "solution," and "call to action." It could be "everyone needs income, now or later," "volatility undermines retirement income," "solutions that reduce volatility." Each section would start with a header that pointed you toward the topic. Emphasizing concision and bullet points, we deliberately prevented it from becoming a script. You'd recognize the presentation, whether you were in Kalamazoo or Costa Mesa; however, each of us would bring our own authentic "voice" and signature to the pitch.

Agenda Stated Upfront

We always let the listener know in advance where the pitch and presentation would be going. Sometimes we would open up the narrative by letting the listener tell us upfront where they wanted to take this communication. It really depended on the setting and context. One inviolate rule—tell the listener upfront what was in store for them, and obtain their permission in the beginning. As one old wag put it, "tell them what you're going to tell the, tell them, and then tell them what you told them."

Opening and Subject

Just as we began with the end in mind, the last part of the process would include boiling the subject down to its most flavorful essence. Keeping it simple, we would open with a short but attention grabbing analogy or metaphor, then quickly pivot to the essence of the subject. After September 11, we opened by referencing Ernest Shackleton's arduous and dangerfilled trek of to the South Pole, a subject that helped clients navigate a period filled with fear and self doubt.

Later, we profiled Julia Morgan—the first female architectural engineer in America, and a designer of buildings that withstood the 1907 San Francisco earthquake. We were reinforcing the importance of building portfolios that could withstand unexpected economic and financial shocks. The idea was to grab people's attention and pivot to the essence of the day's topic. Over the span of thirty years, this process, in one form or another, came to be the armature for the marketing message of AFD. This skeleton helped AFD to raise nearly a trillion dollars in mutual fund assets—not bad for a company that never advertised to the general public. Pretty Zen, if you ask me.

Culture

Culture can reasonably be defined as the way in which people in an organization treat one another. If one single aspect of my eleven years as an associate of the Capital Group stands out, it's my firsthand experience with the healthy and positive culture the Capital leadership has built, beginning in 1933. Defining the culture at Capital became much easier because of the explicit communication that Chairman Jon Lovelace and President Mike Shanahan provided at a series of meetings with the sales force. They knew we spoke to clients every day. They made very sure we understood the culture.

Fair

This is a word that corporate America and many business schools seem to avoid. Not so at Capital. Jon and Mike made sure we understood that being fair to ourselves, our fellow Capital associates, and our clients was paramount.

Fairness started with the very ownership of the company. The Lovelace family began offering their stock to fellow employees for purchase as far back as the 1950s. By the late '90s, over three hundred employees owned stock in the company. Forbes magazine once described Jon as "dumb as a fox." The more stock he sold, the greater the increase in value his fellow owners would create. Zen beautiful, if you ask me.

Of equal importance, both Jon and Mike would sit patiently in front of the sales force, not looking at all like guys worth one billion each. Questions from the sales force seemed to carry a certain charge—either nervousness or a desire to impress that would radiate in the questions to these two. Like Zen masters, their serene demeanor would fill the room with a question in response to a question.

"If we did what you ask, how would we best balance the interests of our clients and work associates?"

"Thank you for your idea. Who should we invite to participate in considering such an idea?"

Capital could make a decision; yet, it rarely made a rash one. If you did make a rash decision, you'd hear about it later. At one point, coaching a sales director, I put together a file of activity and sales data and rushed the job. I didn't make that mistake again. He was off the hook. I'd put myself on the hook and learned the importance of taking the time to work a project thoughtfully and patiently. I learned. We all learned.

Balance

How does an organization provide a sense of balance? First, listening becomes the expected norm. Capital would explicitly expect that everyone listen carefully to one another. Talk about a simple and highly constructive cornerstone to a corporate culture. Respect was another cornerstone: Let's just say, eyerolling would typically earn you a stiff reprimand. Capital also refused to advertise to the public. It would not allow its portfolio counselors and analysts to appear on television and discuss securities we liked or disliked. The younger and newer managers struggled with this cultural loop.

Shanahan and Lovelace made it quite clear. "What we know, we know because of the work we do in exchange for the management fee the shareholders pay us. To give that information and insight away on television creates two problems. We're giving away something that doesn't belong to us. It belongs to the shareholders. Plus, once we put it out on television, it will quickly be baked into the price of the security we're discussing. At that point, it's worthless to the people who paid us for it."

It's hard to describe how antiquated this thinking sounded to newly minted finance mavens, but it perfectly reflected our culture. It explained concisely and persuasively how we differed from most of our competitors.

Listening led naturally to a tenet of making sure the people affected by a decision would be invited to participate in the discussion; the idea was simply that including work associates most familiar with an issue made the decisionmaking process more likely to withstand the test of time. All such simple stuff, yet it provided a sense of balance and equanimity that made employees feel more secure, less stressed, and more able to focus on the task at hand—their job.

Long Term

"Longterm and enduring" became a staple phrase in my vocabulary. Native Americans speak of wise decisions being judged most appropriately over seven generations. Capital would agree. How a decision might play out over time seemed a constant theme and discipline for us as managers.

In a more modern context, economists refer to the Law of Unintended Consequences. This notion went to the heart of many of our discussions about everyday business issues. As an example, we rarely fiddled with compensation. When we did discuss changes, the notion of what we might be missing in our thinking underscored each scenario. How would a salesperson view it? How might they "game" it? Pricing became a constant discussion topic in the late '90s as other fund complexes experimented with B shares and C shares. This became our effort at giving old Joe down south some relief from his calling the brokers "wussies."

As background:

- A shares charge the shareholder upfront for the commission and pay it out at the time of the initial investment.
- B shares charge the shareholder over time (usually five years) but pay the commission to the adviser up front.
- C shares charge the shareholder over a ten-year period and compensate the adviser over the same ten-year period.

As you would expect, Capital was probably the last major fund company to change the pricing of our fund shares. We would watch all the others and only then modify and tweak our pricing accordingly. Our B shares converted to A shares after the redemption period to give shareholders a bit of a break. Similarly, our C shares converted eventually in an effort to encourage long-term investing by being just a bit fairer to long-term fund owners. Fairness, balance, and a long-term view provided the lens for Capital, and it always seemed to hang together.

The idea of long-term, balanced, and fair came into sharp focus one day when the phone rang. An adviser in Detroit, Mike Balagna, called to tell me that he had mailed me a very special prospectus...from 1961. A long-term client of his, an elderly lady, had just died, and her son had asked Mike to come over to her townhouse to help sort through the papers in her investment drawer. There, they found her original prospectus for ICA, the Investment Company of America. In pristine shape, it showed clearly what she had read marked with her underlinings and questions. The son told Mike the original story.

The boy's father had left him and his mom while he was still a baby. In order to make ends meet, she took a job as a secretary at one of the large downtown Detroit banks. Realizing early that her salary left her and her baby with a hand-to-mouth existence, she convinced her mother to watch her son at night while she worked as a cocktail waitress. Working at The Roostertail, a high-roller dinner club, she began to invest her tip money in the fund every month. Putting on fishnet hosiery and serving cocktails provided her enough extra cash to put at least a hundred dollars a week into ICA. She kept it up for seventeen years, until her young son was ready to head off to college.

She graduated to head bartender and kept investing well into her late fifties, when she finally scaled back to just one job. The lady in fishnets paid for her son's college, bought a nice townhouse in Grosse Pointe, and left him with a very nice inheritance when she passed away in 1996. His stepped up tax basis exceeded $2,100,000. Remarkable! She personified everything we stood for at Capital. She kept a long-term view, balanced by a sense of being fair to herself, her son, and future generations.

Former buddies and coworkers tell me that, in recent years, times have changed for Capital. Some of the old keepers of the flame recently retired or passed away. In some ways, we fell victim to our own success. So many of us did well enough financially as investors that the grind of weekly corporate travel no longer made much sense.

Obviously, the 2009 recession also wreaked real havoc on many mutual fund portfolios. Many advisers and their clients—our shareholders—simply couldn't withstand the volatility. In some ways, that period represented one of the only times that Capital's investment record strayed from the "do relatively well in bad markets—valedictorians in summer school" brand. As one old sage put it, "There was simply nowhere to hide."

One other practical reality handicaps former associates and shareholders of the Capital Group as they consider new career opportunities. It's hard to find another company with a culture so thoughtfully constructed and disciplined in its application. Surely, they exist. Yet, most of us found them hard to find and harder to duplicate. As Asian philosophy teaches, "the power of Tao always moves in the direction of returning."

What Jonathan Bell Lovelace and his son, Jon, created at Capital will live on for seven generations—maybe longer. It thrives in each of us who worked there. It thrives in how we live within our families and new organizations, in our charities and politics. In the end, what they created overshadowed the values on a mutual fund statement. These eternal values endure beyond currency—we always sensed that they already knew that.

33
Fridays with Rodriguez

Moving to California as a family in 1997 became easier when our first grader Sam began to read, and all the kids could attend the same school. It happened to be a fairly typical Catholic parish school. Maybe a touch more traditional than most. Sister Ann Bernard O'Shea, (aka Nunzilla) ran the school like an ever present and benevolent dictator. Demanding, exacting and willing to confront any and all transgressions with a cheerful ferocity; parents tended to love Sister Ann. The students not so much. She became my true blue buddy.

My religious education tended to be ad hoc and spotty. Marrying a Catholic in an Episcopal church made my mutt status official. Seeing young Sam take his First Communion began to stir my own spiritual crockpot. Moreover, holding on to some old grudges began to weigh on my conscience. Maybe the time had come to learn about forgiveness. The question would become tangled around who would be forgiving whom and for what. Parsing out the depth of forgiveness would be illuminating. I had very consciously decided to explore the idea of becoming a Catholic.

My first call was to Sister Rita who ran adult religious education for the parish. Diminutive and feisty as a terrier, my work travel regimen couldn't have mattered less to this lady tasked with saving adult souls across the parish. She simply informed me that I must not be serious if I would let a little detail like my job interfere with my spiritual awakening. Traveling for work Monday through Thursday could be described as nonnegotiable as a sales manager for the American Funds. I let Sister Rita know I needed to think over the challenge of attending religious instruction every Wednesday evening over a ten month period. She smiled the smile of a pain in the ass who had just been awarded Round One.

The following Friday my being in town allowed me to pick up the kids from the school. A treat I looked forward to all week. As the kids and I walked across the playground to my car, Sister Ann waved firmly at me. As she approached, she suggested to the kids that they go on to the car. The kids had already focused on the refuge of my car in case one of them had unknowingly incurred the wrath of Nunzilla. She surprised me as she began gently.

"I heard about your conversation with Sister Rita."

"Did I make the grade for dinner table conversation at the Rectory?" I asked with a smile.

"Let me suggest you meet with Monsignor Rodriguez. He lives up at the Sand Hill Rectory next to St. Denis."

She offered all of this guidance with the certainty of the Head of School and the daughter of a police captain from the Mission neighborhood of San Francisco. She had tended bar at O'Shea's prior to becoming a nun. She went from helping with her family's business to helping with the needs of all her families. She was a Corker. I don't know if I ever liked someone so much who rarely smiled or laughed.

Apart from my tending bar at the faculty/clergy clambake, my employer and I provided new computers for the school tech lab. She was generous and shrewd all at the same time. Trusting her implicitly, I called Monsignor John Rodriguez.

Monsignor of the St. Denis Parish via the Catholic Universities of both Manila and Washington D.C., John

Rodriguez had been the second born son on a Spanish farm near the Pyrenees and the French border. An area dominated by low lying farms where historically herders would move their cows and sheep to higher, cooler meadows in summer. Living in cool stone summer cottages, the transhumance nature of his young life influenced John deeply. The French city of Lourdes with its healing waters sat on the eastern side of the Pyrenees and irrigated spiritual life across the hundreds of parishes and communities on both the Spanish and French side of these rugged mountains. With primogeniture assigning the farm to John's elder brother, he settled early on the priesthood as his calling. His mother's daily Mass kept him early and often at her side. The Catholic Church became his home.

John took his studies very seriously and eventually earned a PhD in Ethics and Religion which opened the door to his teaching duties in both Manila and Washington. Immediately before his elevation to Monsignor for St. Denis, he served the homeless, drug addicts and sex workers in the "Tenderloin" of San Francisco. By the time my lost soul called him on the phone, he'd pretty much seen it all. Rich and poor, gay and straight, healthy and ill, he served his Lord as the spirit appeared directly in front of him. His calm demeanor could not be cracked. He listened with an intensity I'd never witnessed. He made space for others that they didn't know they had. He may be the first and only Holy Man I've ever known.

He knew my call was coming, and he seemed very ready.

"This travel schedule is pretty heavy?" he gently probed.

"Pretty much Monday through Thursday, most weeks." I conceded.

"Do you like coffee? Really good coffee…?" he asked almost playfully. "Sure! I pretty much live on the stuff…" I said mostly to keep things light.

"Great!! Bring two cups of the best you can find this Friday and we'll talk", he offered.

"8:00 okay?" I said mostly trying to honor my work duties on my official office day.

"Perfect, I live in the Rectory next to St. Denis." sealing the deal.

For a forty year old man who bounced from one church to the next as a boy, this seemed almost like wiping the slate clean. Plus, if it worked out well, I could attend Mass with my kids and take Communion as the father in our family. It felt like making a new start. Unprepared as I was for what lay in store, I was excited.

As I drove up to St. Denis and the Rectory, I could see John standing in his front doorway.

"Welcome, welcome….ah!!!…your coffee smells wonderful! Thank you!"

Such a welcome as we entered his Rectory home and settled into two very comfortable but somewhat spartan chairs around a large coffee table. His questions came slowly and firmly. Tell me about your wife. Your children. He asked about my mother's experience teaching at the Catholic school in the Bahamas. He probed a little more determinedly around my father and our inactive relationship. All the ground you would expect to cover, we covered it. Finally, he handed me "the book". This was not the Bible. "The Catechism of the Catholic Church" written by John Paul II became our preferred method of instruction.

He simply asked if reading 50-60 pages a week would be reasonable? At that moment, I realized for the first time that this would be one on one instruction. He never said it out loud. He would be guiding me personally through the Catholic faith. Teacher and pupil, priest and soul, we were about to become a team.

> The Church believes the Nicene Creed.
> The Church celebrates the Sacraments.
> The Church lives the Commandments.
> The Church prays the Lord's Prayer.

Each of the four elements took a couple of months. We started with nearly a month on the concept of "free will". Coming from a family of libertarian subversives, this was an important first intellectual hurdle. You cannot sin if your do not have free will. When the government has a gun to your head, sinning or being virtuous doesn't count. This hit home big time for me. It help me parse out genuine goodness from the phony mercenary kind. In our family, this theme resonated from my Grandma Sally to my mom and directly to me. Grandma used to say she didn't care for "churchy people". I could tell Monsignor Rodriguez felt very much the same way. This began to feel right.

So, it started. Every Friday morning I would bring two cups of coffee from Peet's Coffee on Santa Cruz Boulevard in Menlo Park. Monsignor and I would tackle the Nicene Creed line by line. He explained the Sacraments and their significance. Saints kept us busy toward the end for a solid month and half. In time, as Lent approached the Catechism began to run its course. Finally, he threw me a curve ball.

"What kind of books do you like to read?"

"Economics and golf mostly…" I burped naively.

"No! No! I mean spiritual books. What kind of spiritual books do you like?" he emphasized.

"Oh…I'm not sure", that was a toughie. After all, I couldn't lie to a Priest?

His eyes never wavered. "Come on, there must be one?" he repeated.

"Ok, I read this one book. 'Tuesdays with Morrie', would that count?

"Okay, maybe…what can you tell me about it?" he seemed intrigued.

So, I began to lay out the storyline. Morrie Schwartz was Mitch Albom's favorite college professor. They'd lost touch with one another. It had been more than 20 years. They reconnected over Morrie's illness. Mitch started a pattern of visiting his old professor every Tuesday until he passed. The lessons seemed eternal. Monsignor said he'd give the book a try.

The next Friday, Monsignor Rodriguez again stood in his front doorway waiting to greet me with the declaration, "this is like Scripture!" Sure enough, the last few weeks consisted mostly of our exploration of the Mitch Albom theme that death may be the end of a life but not necessarily the end of the relationship. Mitch would still connect with Morrie after he passed away. "Afterlife" took on new meaning. It operated in memory and dreams and remembrances. Ultimately, we chose what to hold on to with our loved ones. We chose whether those remembrances darken us or lighten us.

"Death marks the end of a life, but not the end of the relationship".

I couldn't help but remind myself of the father I found so hard to forgive. He would, in fact, someday die. If I were going to learn how to forgive him, I better get on with it. I might be running out of time.

Catholics believe that confession and forgiveness changes us. It does not change God. God forgives us through the Calvary of Jesus on the Cross. The difficult question arises when we consider the act of forgiving someone who does not acknowledge their "trespasses". Sometimes those that trespass against us don't even realize they're trespassing. Even while they're trespassing, they don't see their conduct objectively. It's as if their self-defeating behavior sits in their own personal blind spot.

How do we forgive the unrepentant? How does that work? John made it simple. Forgive them anyway. Tell them you forgive them. Make space for their righteous indignation and forgive them for that as well.

I will say. It worked. My father treated my mother poorly. He treated my brother poorly. Eventually, he even treated me poorly. Although he could not understand why I forgave him, it didn't matter. I stuck to my guns. Made space for his indignation and simply said, "dad, I forgive you for all of it". I'm moving on and letting it all go. Forgiving him became the precursor for allowing me to let go.

I could see my own actions more clearly once I forgave him. How meshed into my accusations lay a set of expectations that I put on dad that he may not have fully intended to accept. I trusted him too much. I wanted him to look out for me, and then stood poised for outrage when he let me down. My own behavior began to look very self-defeating and childlike with the benefit of hindsight sprinkled heavily with forgiveness.

That made my forty Fridays with Rodriguez worth it right there. Dropping my anger helped me and everyone around me. It lightened my heart, and my mood. It lifted one more stone off my soul.

At this point, my relationship with Monsignor began to evolve. As I let go of charged emotions and made my own confession, space opened up in my heart to be more generous to John. One day, he asked me.

"Where do you want to take your First Communion?
"Do you want a private service with just your family?"
I hadn't thought about it. It was a little unexpected.

He was genuinely asking me and it sounded like a completely open question. With my new found spiritual space, I instead asked him a question. I asked a question that I would not have made space for ten months earlier.

"Monsignor, you're in the business of saving souls. Where do you want to have it?"

He made an incredibly generous ten month investment of time in one lost soul. He had helped me reclaim my spirit and sense of purpose. It was time for him to be rewarded, not me. So, I transposed the question to him instead.

He simply said, "would Pentecostal Sunday be okay?"

I thought to myself. "Shit, did I miss that chapter?. So soon? What the hell is Pentecostal Sunday? Does this involve those snakes and tongues of fire?"

Instead I asked, "can we go over that again? What's this Pentecostal Sunday all about?"

Monsignor patiently reviewed that Jesus prophesied his return as the Holy Spirit and the beginning of the Church. He reminded me that ancient scripture described the psychological and spiritual overhaul that the disciples experienced metaphorically with strong winds and heat as fire lashing their minds. The Holy Spirit overcame the fear within the disciples and gave them the gift of communication. This Sabbath day in Church when the disciples burst forward to spread the Word - Catholics know this day as Pentecostal Sunday.

Well I was not about to stand in the way of that kind of significance. As a new Catholic, this sounded like more than a good enough day to kick off my new spiritual life. As a sales and marketing guy with a love for great communication, this might just be the perfect day for me to confess my faith. With my family around me, and as part of the packed church at the 9:30 Mass, I welcomed Christ into my life as a forty year old man.

Monsignor still had one spiritual trick up his sleeve. His homily that day would, of course, emphasize that our lives, our deeds and our openness carries forward the Holy Spirit to others. He laid out how a single life can influence others when it brings significance and meaning. This homily flowed directly into the storyline of "Tuesdays with Morrie". He captured so snugly the beautiful life of this charming professor at Brandeis and his relationship with Mitch Albom. How Morrie Schwartz' lifetime of relationships positively influenced the hundreds of lives he touched.

Most unexpectedly, Monsignor then began to describe how that happened between him and me. In front of this full house Mass at St. Denis in Menlo Park, California on Pentecostal Sunday, he laid out our story. Conveying to the parish that our relationship, in fact, improved both of us. Needless to say, I was not ready for this nuance. He announced to the world. We have "Tuesdays with Morrie" and now we have for eternity "Fridays with Rodriguez".

A few weeks later, I walked down Santa Cruz Avenue for my morning breakfast at Ann's Coffee Shop. Suddenly, a voice boomed from across the street, "Hey! Fridays with Rodriguez!". I waved back to a man I didn't recognize and did not know. It was perfect.

34

Gift from God

In the Old Testament, Hannah and Elkanah conceived a child. She asked God for this gift. 1 Samuel 1:20 tells us that the Lord gave onto them this gift, and from this child, a lifetime of lessons and insights flowed to them. Samuel provided just such a joyful and humbling stream of gifts to our family.

This is that story.

Marriage intimidated me from the very beginning. The responsibility and sense of duty often overwhelmed me. Maybe, most men feel this anxiety. I sure did. My own parents' divorce added to the apprehension. As unexpected as our third born, Samuel, was for me, his arrival transcended those fears, almost from the very beginning.

He made me a better person, husband and father in important ways. Learning the true meaning of unconditional love arose from how Sam challenged his nursery, kindergarten and primary school teachers. His presence reminded me that actions speak louder than words, particularly as a husband and as an example to our children. Ultimately, I came to realize that my own foibles and flaws bore the same self-examination I expected of my grown children. An important lesson I learned late in life.

"I cannot hear your words. Your actions speak too loudly" -

Sam set a local record for close calls on school discipline matters. If you "rate what you skate", as the Navy likes to say, Sam skated close to three school departures and one suspension. Two in nursery school, one in second grade and one near miss during his junior year of high school. How can a dad not love a kid who survives so many close calls? With a mixture of bemusement and irreverent pride, each near crash and burn with the school leadership wedded me more closely to our little Sambo. He was a charmer, no question about it.

It's said that Albert Einstein and Thomas Edison didn't speak until they hit their fifth birthdays. A good reminder when your son cannot talk, but decides instead to use his fists to communicate. Probably by overreacting to a crayon theft by a fellow nursery school chum, Sam found his right hook his most effective tool of persuasion. The nursery school teachers disagreed.

When you're young parents, and the teachers tell you, "you really should have him professionally tested..." —your heart skips a beat. Topped by cowlicks sprouting in multiple directions, he just seemed to be growing at many different speeds all at the same time. The words just didn't arrive with the rest of him. The testing told us why.

At age five, he could assemble puzzles and wooden block games meant for ten and eleven year olds. Ask him to describe what he did...nothing but a big grin! Between an older brother, sister, mother, father and four grandparents who did EVERYTHING for him, why talk? Everything was done for him with a mere grunt and a point. Compounding matters, both his parents tended to speak at machine gun pace, particularly when trying to manage the chaos of three kids 46 months apart. Who could blame him? He occupied a front row seat in a junior madhouse that also endured three corporate re-locations during the same 46 months.

We all slowed down our speech. We stopped waiting on him hand and foot. We spoke more clearly, explicitly and less figuratively. In six months, everything was fine. Two school departures avoided. Sambo moved on to kindergarten...barely.

"Reading is fundamental" –

Second grade for Sam meant a mid year move from Ann Arbor to Menlo Park, California. Providentially, only the St. Raymond's Catholic parish school would accept all three siblings in January as we moved into our new Bay Area home. Sure enough, the bouncing from one nursery school to another and a new kindergarten left Sam missing one important second grade skill. He couldn't read. The semi-benevolent nun Sister Ann Bernard O'Shea pronounced Sam unable to stay because he couldn't read the workbooks they used for their second grade instruction. "Nunzilla" as the kids nicknamed her, made it so. Only my negotiating a three week stay of execution prevented it from being immediately enforced.

So, we taught Sam to read in three weeks. Believe me, this says far more about the quality of his mind than the quality of our instruction. Only knowing phonics as a method for teaching, Annie and I dutifully sat with Sam after school and during the evenings as he learned to sound out the letters and combinations. English with all of its overlapping homonyms and synonyms revealed itself to us as one very difficult language to teach, much less read and write. Yes, it's rich in vocabulary and diction. However, it's very tough to learn to read...in just three weeks.

Yet, Sam learned it well enough to remain. Sister Ann gave him his reprieve, and Sam stayed in the same school as his two siblings. Disaster averted.

Something important happened during our little trial by fire. Sam wandered onto my lap one night as I sat reading in front of our old California clinker brink style fireplace. He laid his little head on my shoulder and we both stared into the fire. Four eyes lost in the flames and embers.

"Dad, can I ask you a question?"
"Sure Sam, what's on your mind?"
"Dad, do you remember Ann Arbor?"
"Yes, Sam I do"
"Dad, so do I…"

My heart sank. We'd only been gone for six weeks. In his young mind, that seemed like an eternity. Worse yet, I underestimated the impact of the move. He was that unhappy.

I knew my attachment to Ann Arbor ran deep. It never occurred to me that little Sam might feel the loss as much or more than me. In fact, I'd been so preoccupied with leaving my home, my mom, my lifelong friends, I'd neglected to consider how the move had affected the kids, especially the youngest, little Sambo. Shame on me! I'd missed something very big.

I learned that being a father meant more than providing a comfortable home, a good school, and a safe neighborhood. I'd forgotten to listen, really actively listen. A mistake I tried hard not to repeat.

"Packing tartar sauce in his backpack"

"Kirk, you just need to accept the fact that he's too small…" How many football players and parents listen to that superficial observation and make a choice? Some move on to baseball, basketball or other sports. Some use those dismissive words as rocket fuel. Sam chose the later. For the next nine years, football became Sam's passion. Every time a coach slighted him or accorded him too little respect, Sam just topped off his own personal rocket fuel tank. Then, he shocked them all.

One year, the homecoming game for the other team gave Sam a chance at middle linebacker to take out their first and second team tailbacks on successive clean, very hard hits. When their third stringer woozily staggered back to the huddle, the referee puts his arm around Sam, "I cannot call a penalty on you son, but how about you just dial it down a bit, okay?" At 5' 9" and 190, he just willed himself to All-Conference and academic honors, team MVP, and the special award for Most Courageous Player in the program. All of this from the kid they said was too small, too slow and too academic.

In high school, Sam found one more way to defeat the "too small" skeptics. He discovered wrestling. Boy, did he discover it. Competing only against wrestlers all of the same weight meant he could really shine. Shined his way to the New England Prep title at 164 lbs. Adding a second place in the Easterns, he qualified for the National Prep tourney at Lehigh University in Pennsylvania. This tournament included wrestlers from parochial and private high schools across the eastern two thirds of the country, and meant he could wrestle the great Eddie Ruth.

Winning his first two matches handily, he went ahead 9-2 in his quarterfinal match. Then, disaster struck. We didn't know watching from the stands, because he hid it so well. He started drooping his left arm. In fact, it drooped because he dislocated his elbow. Can you imagine? He actually dislocated his elbow. It's just painful to write about or say out loud. What really amazed his mother and me. He kept on wrestling in the match.

The momentum of the match swung the other way. 9-2 became 12-6, then 13-9, then 14-12 and it looked like he was bound to lose. Then, the son of a gun just generated one last take down with his good arm, and won the damn match 15-12. When the ref tried to raise his left arm in victory, his knees buckled and the coach and team doctor leapt onto the mat. With their shoulders under each of his arms, they carried him to a training bed behind a curtain meant for injured wrestlers. Fighting back tears, he pleaded for the coach to let him keep wrestling. Obviously, that was not going to happen. The only winning logic I could muster, "Sam, when you're old and gray sitting on the front porch with your grandchildren, you can tell them you were UNDEFEATED in the National Prep tourney...." He actually smiled and finally conceded that he was done. One of the few times, in fact, that he ever conceded anything. Plus, he did not have to wrestle Ed Ruth.

We see what we want to see.

His college recommendation from that high school included the phrase, "send this kid after Moby Dick and he packs tartar sauce in his backpack..." You can see why. Overcoming a childhood and adolescence being told that he wasn't good enough, tall enough or smart enough, he marched off to college at the University of Michigan. It's said that adversity is a gift. If we view adversity as a gift, Sam lived that concept almost every day. He taught me so very, very much.

As a Wolverine, he followed in the footsteps of his big sister, brother, cousins, parents, uncles and aunts. Even his grandmother and great grandmother could smile down on their little Sambo. He was happy and proud—but not half as much as his mother and father, and loving family.

Recently, Sam finished serving as a lieutenant in the United States Navy. After finishing a tough deployment on the USS Harper's Ferry, this Assistant Engineer recently married the love of his life. Without a doubt, he will bring to his marriage and family that same optimism, open mindedness and passion that served him so well as a boy and young man.

At our recent Christmas dinner, we found ourselves reminiscing about a family favorite, the movie "White Christmas". Between spoonfuls of Christmas fettuccine, we resurrected the sentimental scenes with Bing Crosby and Rosemary Clooney. Sam asked me why I love the movie so much? Is it the sentimental idea of Christmas. I thought awhile before answering.

Actually, two scenes stand out from the others for me. First, when "Bob Wallace" and "Betty Haynes" sing *Count Your Blessings* to each other, I'm fixated. If one song could capture the unsentimental but positive ethos of my typical American family, it's that song. Americans know we to be a blessed people. Not because of race or religion, wealth or status, we're blessed because we know that such genuine humility will raise us as a people, as families, and as Americans. Genuine unsentimental humility is a true gift whether you're Bing Crosby or Condi Rice or Sambo.

The other scene that puts broad grins on movie audiences starts with the Mary Wickes character "Emma Allen" eavesdropping on a phone call at the Inn. Bing's character is trying in this phone call to sell "Ed Harrison" (Sullivan) to let him come on the show and pitch some old soldiers into coming to this struggling Vermont ski resort and provide a grand tribute to their former Army General and hero. She only hears fragments of the conversation. So, naturally she misunderstands. What's so subtle is how she misunderstands in a way that belies what she herself is really thinking. She pities the general and feels sorry for him. Therefore, her misunderstanding lays all of that onto Bing's character. Scotoma comes from the Greek word for the medical condition related to a gap or filtering of a person's vision. Metaphorically, it describes the tendency, based on partial consideration of what's present, to only see what the mind wants to see.

Sam and I chuckled as we thought about the movie and how humanity often stumbles into the same partial perceptions of what's going on around us. Scotoma remains more common than most of want to admit. We "know" something. We tend to identify people and behavior that fits into what we "know". With the onset of social media, it's both harder on our senses and easier to fit ourselves inside the echo chambers that reinforce what we know.

With Sam's decision to not accept the Navy retention bonus, he enrolled in the Annenberg School of Journalism at the University of Southern California. He describes in such detail how he's learning the craft of reporting events accurately and with an eye for the underlying reason an event occurs. His observations run the gamut from the coverage of athletic competitions in former Soviet block countries to the Winter

Olympics in Korea. Based just south of the DMZ and the drama in North Korea, he could see how sports and politics blur into a conflagration where all sides "see what they want to see". Just along for the ride, this becomes the most enjoyable part of parenthood. For him to see in his twenties what took me fifty years to decipher means he really does stand on the shoulders of all of us.

Sam has been one of my greatest teachers. Truly, he lives the name—"Gift from God".

35

Character Spaghetti

Admiring someone can be tricky business. They can disappoint you sometimes. Connie Restuccia never disappoints me. Over 40 years, her story just gets better and better.

"I set my alarm clock for twelve midnight."

Connie was premed and straight A's. She knew with her deep Sicilian roots and uncles who took 3-5 year vacations under federal roof, there were only two ways to avoid the family business. She could become a nun or a doctor. Wanting to be a doctor and wanting to play doctor are not quite the same thing. She wanted her freedom and planned on being a mom. She chose medicine as a career in order to secure her own life mask, and just as importantly freedom for her children.

Connie played tennis in high school, but not well enough to play college tennis. So, she did the next best thing. She dated the star of the tennis team who happened to look like a 6' 3" version of Andy Garcia from Godfather III. When this Mediterranean Adonis came to her father's home to pick her up for a summertime date of baseball and burgers, he received a bit of a shock.

First, driving down Lakeview Drive brought our Medonis to a street number not on a mailbox but beautifully painted on a high wall with a gate. Pulling through the gate, he proceeded up the long driveway to park just in front of a large stone mansion with an equally impressive front door. The Sicilian butler doubled as security. He invited our young olive skinned Medonis inside and grunted.

"Mr. Vinnie wants to meet you.." as he pointed toward the dark wood paneled study.

A family home for a Sicilian father bulks up with lots of children, including some grown children. Medonis absorbed it all as he slowly strode into the dark study staring at the walls filled with ecclesiastical Italian art. He knew enough to sit up straight in the high wingback leather chair across from Mr. Vinnie's oversized desk.

When Mr. Vinnie arrived in his silk jacket and jet black hair, he made pleasantries Palermo style.

"So, you're the big tennis star?"

Medonis nodded warily, "well, I play on our team. Yes sir."

"Yea, so you college boys are very smart. This is how this is going to work. I set my alarm clock for twelve midnight. You two go have fun. You come back here. You enjoy the view of the lake. You drink some soda pop. But, I DO NOT WANT TO HEAR MY ALARM GO OFF…"

"Capisce? We understand each other?"

Medonis starts nodding as he catches on…quickly.

"Got it, we go to the ballgame but we're back here before midnight and we turn off that alarm clock."

"You college boys are smart".

Medonis checked his wristwatch regularly every inning that night—very regularly.

Medonis and Connie only dated a few more times. But, he always remembered to bring her back early enough to turn off that alarm. Many pundits credit Mr. Vinnie with arranging to have a few double crossers dropped down incinerator smokestacks.

"Doesn't miss much."

Connie graduated pre-med summa cum laude which is Latin for "doesn't miss much". Her grades and MCAT score earned her admission to George Washington University School of Medicine.

There, she befriended one of the Kennedy clan. Similarly, this young nephew of Senator Ted Kennedy did not want to join his family's business of American politics. They became fast friends. Socializing with the Kennedy clan could only be described as joining the A team. Handsome young American elite working hard and playing hard, most every weekend.

One particularly raucous weekend found them with young Ted Kennedy, Jr. and John Kennedy, Jr. sailing the "Honey Fitz" near Annapolis on the Chesapeake Bay. Ted Jr. overcame a cancerous osteosarcoma in his leg which led to an amputation at age 12. John Jr. lost his dad at age three in a cataclysmic American event that he never fully understood, and the rest of the world would struggle for years to understand. Connie said it best. John-John used his natural manifold and understated people skills to charm nearly everyone deserving of that famous Kennedy spell.

When it came to the cousins Ted Jr. and John Jr., the practical jokes and horseplay reached their zenith during those post college days. Young, unmarried and wealthy, they didn't worry about much, or taking things too far. Ted's prosthetic leg was almost too tempting a toy for his cousins looking for some extra fun and hijinks. It wasn't a question of if the leg would go missing. It was only a matter of when and how. How could John-John pass up a boozy overnight boat cruise. Perfect timing.

Once the late night drinking maxed out, Ted Jr. found the sleeping berth below deck and passed out cold. John-John quietly and gently removed Ted's leg, threw it over his shoulder, and took it topside. He found a small inflatable raft with an extra long line running from a stern cleat to the raft... with the leg secured inside the raft. Every raft needs a rudder. Floating some 100' feet behind the boat, this raft with only a leg to steer it made quite a sight...all night...until morning. Connie told me the morning wake up call from Ted Jr. was damn loud and very clear.

"Who took my fucking leg????" provided the morning alarm bell for the nautical revelers.

Connie said it best. John Jr. would have entered politics with a very, very high ceiling.

"Doctor Restuccia, we have a collect call for you..."

Connie settled on interventional radiology for her residency. She moved back to Michigan and finished her training at the large University Hospital in Ann Arbor. In less than ten years, she chaired the Radiology Department. This role led to running the monthly meeting with specialty department heads. A meeting that focused on evaluating and discussing the most challenging cases in the hospital at any given time. Connie earned her promotion. Her peers heading up the department viewed her as a true up and comer. She rose to department chair pretty rapidly. All of which made this phone call a bit of a shock.

"Dr. Restuccia, we have an unusual phone call for you" said the receptionist bluntly as she entered the hospital conference room just before the weekly CR meeting.

"It's a collect call from your Uncle Dante at the Merion Federal Penitentiary...". The department heads looked up from the files on the large table in front of them. They looked at one another with a quizzical look. A couple managed a smile.

Connie worked up a weak smile of her own. She looked her colleagues squarely in the eye and said simply, "Gentlemen, that's a call I'm going to need to take."

Never complain, never explain. Connie kept it short and simple.

I asked what Dante actually wanted. She told me he'd been working on his golf tan at this federal facility, and thought he might have a little skin cancer. He wanted her to check him once they released him. Turned out, he was released into witness protection. Living in some remote Southern California Inland Empire suburb, everything was fine until they found the body. Dante wasn't even sure which body the FBI found. It was one too many. Dante went back under federal roof for another 5-7. Every family has their stories. Connie just seemed to own a few more.

"Doctor Restuccia, this is the manager of the ice rink. There's been an accident."

Connie shuttered as she listened to this phone call. Being a doctor she knew when calls seemed most ominous. This was one of those calls.

Connie's husband of 25 years playing Beer League hockey took a check from behind and crashed head first into the boards. Already heading to the emergency room, Connie caught up to Joe and the ER staff about 20 minutes after his arrival. As she feared, the initial diagnosis confirmed paralysis—a loss of use of the upper arms and shoulders, but not complete paralysis of the hands and fingers. Neurosurgeons call it "surfer in a barrel". The C vertebrae are damaged, but the actual spinal cord is not severed. As the early days passed, the prognosis evolved from incredibly grim to somewhat grim. There was hope.

As Connie recounted these events to me over coffee one long morning, I noticed under her blouse an elaborate undershirt and camisole. Her details of Joe and his months of physical therapy made my mind wonder just a bit. Finally, I hazarded the question.

"Is this the only close call that you and Joe faced as a married couple?"

Looking from dark green eyes, very intent but with a calm and cool confidence, she hushed:

"Not really, I underwent a double mastectomy two and a half years ago."

Able to self diagnose and because of a fellow radiology oncologist, she had an early indication that there might be trouble. She made the tough decision rationally and promptly. Most of her friends and colleagues never knew about the breast cancer until much later. The surgeon removed all of the cancerous tissue and both breasts. She made the courageous and conservative decision. She made it with complete dignity.

Never complain, never explain.

Mystery solved, I thought to myself if there is one person in this world I could reliably admire, it would be Connie Restuccia. If life is a series of ups and downs, few people I'd ever known over a long stretch of time could compare to Connie. Every shit sandwich life fed her, she flicked away with grace and dignity, class and character.

Eventually, with Connie and his former colleagues guiding his neurological recovery, Joe could walk the dog, and ride a bicycle for miles at a time. He did give up his license as a doctor. He did show similar levels of grit and determination as we'd all seen in Connie. They really were meant for each other. Still, we all knew she was the Madrina who guided this family. She gave new meaning to what it meant to be the leader of a family, the spiritual depth and breadth of family.

Seeing through the noise of American life, it can be challenging to see all the good around us. Often it doesn't come neat and tidy. It can be politically very incorrect. Identity politics becomes an useful excuse for not understanding individuals and the choices they're forced to make. Goodness should not be mistaken for sanitized clean artificial lives. Goodness often looks more like spaghetti than Neapolitan ice cream.

It's authentic, lofty and low, all at the same time. It is, in fact, beautiful beyond measure.

36
Love Letter to Roy

air! You know what fair is? It's cotton candy and Ferris wheels." Or so an old boss used to tell us…and his kids…and anyone else who would listen. It's almost as if "fair" has become a word we now try to avoid. Using it implies a certain naïveté or lack of hardened maturity. Something tells me we might need a better definition of fair, particularly given the contradictions and subtleties of the modern world.

Long ago, American culture mastered the art of speaking out of both sides of its mouth. We tell the world that our constitution provides the framework for citizens to remain free, except for that power which we give over to the government. Yet any discussion of slowing increases in government largesse to our citizens degrades the debate pretty quickly. Talk about slowing the benefit stream of Social Security or entitlements triggers an immediate backlash of "that wouldn't be fair!"

As an undergrad at the University of Colorado, I took classes taught by Kenneth Boulding in Transfer Economics and the Economics of Discrimination and Public Finance. This was heady stuff for the young people of the Front Range, who fancied themselves gurus in cycling, mountaineering, organic foodstuffs, and yoga. Daydreaming in the sunny mountains came to an abrupt end one day in the form of a simple but clever question, "If we're serious about equal opportunity and fairness, shouldn't we allow children to pick their parents?"

Our local Nobel nominee had our attention. We were going downtown, where the poor people live—or, in the case of my hometown of Detroit, barely subsist. Ken knew economics. He had studied at Cambridge under and alongside Sir John Maynard Keynes. While not my favorite economist, Keynes was knighted by the Brits. Keynes knew the subject cold—maybe a little too cold to advance the question Ken asked. Ken took us into the world of microanalytic economics.

In this intellectual neighborhood, we used economic and quantitative tools to break down data and better understand why the human condition includes so many fucked up situations. I loved this stuff. I loved that it made marginal functions and calculus useful for a change. Instead of occupying our time with GNP and money supply estimates, we used linear regression to look for correlations between variables—correlations that might lead to causation.

Pondering Ken's question quickly elucidates a very basic reality: life isn't fair. As much as we want people to be treated fairly, we know the answer after one drive through the poverty of Appalachia or a scant review of college matriculation rates for high schools like Richmond High near Oakland, California. Born there, you need to be Dolly Parton or Coach Carter to make it out and up. Statistically, it's a long shot—with the emphasis on long: like from one end of the basketball court to the other. If you really picture those young faces, it breaks your heart. Even if you're a coldhearted, analytical, microeconomist, it really breaks your heart.

Recently, I welcomed my first Great Godchild. It's hard to capture in words how joyful it makes you. Despite his early challenges, I couldn't help but think of his promising future and the good fortune of his parents, his grandparents, and even of great grandmother GiGi. No dark tunnel empty of light and opportunity for Roy. No. This kid was born on third base, like his Great Godfather. Lord willing, he won't think he hit a triple.

Exploring the meaning of fairness, in a nutshell, is this story.

Fair to One's Self

Let's begin with the hardest of all versions of fair. Fairness to one's self requires the most thorough, thoughtful, and painful kind of introspection—the kind of introspective work that usually translates into a series of emotional "revisits" and a teary investment of time and energy.

Various disciplines in psychiatry and counseling emphasize the need to revisit trauma from earlier in life—often childhood—and look at the events with a more rational adult perspective. Many cultural traditions include this kind of exploration.

Catholics understand it as confession, important enough to make it one of the seven sacraments. Zen Masters take students to an inner state of serenity, free of regret, outward symbols, and attachments. Hebrews speak of viddiu, a verb describing a confession that is inward and private, not a show to others. In a modern context, advances by traumatologists treating victims and witnesses to natural and manmade disasters have begun to make a subtle distinction in the targeting and nature of this revisiting process.

Their methodology takes the client to the specifics of the actual trauma through the human senses. How did it look? What did you hear? How did it smell? Anything taste different in your mouth? These sensory memories can often help trigger the relevant subconscious file holding the full details of the event. Repeating it again and again helps. Making it as vivid and short in duration as possible also helps the patient not just remember it, but reexperience it from a safer distance. Instead of curling up on the floor in the fetal position, the patien goes back to the details of the episode with a healthy insight into the shame, embarrassment, and pain. Tears flow without a fullscale meltdown.

Every day, somewhere in the world, an adult roughs up a child. Sometimes it's physical, but often it's mental. Sadly, we know that it's also often sexual in nature. Whatever the root cause, the human mind (especially the young mind) often cannot properly parse out blame and responsibility. A young mind owns the memory file and the shame, but it's hard to separate the event from our own considerations. Fusing shame or embarrassment or arousal to an episode often gives the memory its charge.

My confusion blurred an afternoon in the Boulder Hospital emergency room into a night with a cop tapping a flashlight into the chest of good buddy. Two different events created the fused memory, but it started with the trauma of a car hitting me and the shady connections between the cops and the joyriding kids who ran me down. I didn't understand the charge, which led to my fist hitting that cop's jaw. Once the memory file was vivid in my mind once again, I could untangle the tightly wound ball of emotional string.

All of us know friends, family members, and coworkers who can't get out of their own way. They bring a pentup energy or charge to their interactions and make the same misjudgments again and again. Actions such as overreacting to a slight or a snub; telling inappropriate jokes in the wrong settings; shading the truth when it's pointless or meaningless. Invariably, these actions carry this behavior from events long ago. The original episodes can look trivial and almost comical in retrospect. In order to be fair to ourselves, we need to revisit them. We need to allow ourselves to feel a measure of the original shame or regret and let the tears flow. Then we can dry the tears; let ourselves off the hook; give ourselves a fair shake; and move on.

Fair to Family

"Sorry I haven't lived up to your expectations." Hearing that from Dad for the first time, I didn't quite know what to make of it. As I thought about it and repeated it a few times, it struck me as meaning much more than meets the eye. I didn't know if it was a real apology, or whether he was just subtly suggesting that our differences might be more about me than him. Clever guy, that old Dad. He knew that for our relationship to work—for any relationship to work—both people need to understand their own expectations.

Modern families face a myriad of challenges: marriage, childbirth, death, health both physical and mental, career choices, crime…You name it, families deal with it every day. So many books start with death. It's odd, if you ask me. Why wouldn't we start with birth? I get the concept of ending on a high note, but how about starting and ending on a high note?

My godson Ross married Karen Hoagland, a smart, confident and a little bit plucky young lady he met while an undergrad at Auburn University. Ross strikes his family and friends as wise beyond his years. Very measured and temperate, he earned the "Plainsman" honor in his senior year at Auburn. This even tempered young man found Karen completely irresistible and loved her sassy style. I think they conceived on their three week honeymoon. Hearing about the honeymoon soon became drowned out by early reports of morning sickness. The idea of a newborn baby made us happy beyond words. Yet, I could sense that Ross' father, my good friend from investment days, began to worry. Intuitively, he knew something was wrong.

Turns out the morning sickness was not a three or four week nuisance. It became an everyday reality. Hyperemesis gravidarum (HG) occurs to varying degrees in many pregnancies. It's estimated that at least 60,000 cases of HG occur annually. Probably more since many women gut it out at home. In Karen's case, workdays became untenable. Sitting at her desk for extended periods proved too much. Late in the second month of her pregnancy, she requested and was granted a partially paid leave of absence. Her small start-up firm simply could not afford to be more accommodating.

At the very time Karen should have been gaining weight, she was losing weight. Twice during the first trimester, Ross checked her into the local hospital so that she could receive fluids and nutrition intravenously. During her third stay, doctors began nasogastric feeding through a tube. My good friend and his son did everything they could. Still, the growing frequency of her hospital stays seemed ominous. Her hormone readings rose to alarming levels. Doctors seemed perplexed to explain why. Late in the second trimester, all hell broke loose.

First, the doctors determined that Karen's estrogen counts reached unsafe levels, contributing to her HG and discomfort. She showed signs of hypertension. Her eyesight seem impacted at times. Sure enough, Karen had developed preeclampsia. In addition, the baby now seemed to be stressed. In the 29th week, her obstetrician decided that delivering the baby by caesarean section very early would be the only alternative.

Roy entered the world well before he or anyone else was ready. He was really tiny. He weighed 750 grams. Very sick from the onset, he endured five blood transfusions and four resuscitations. Calling this kid stubborn and brave hardly seems enough. Seeing the power of the human spirit in such a tiny little guy humbles you to the core. Our drive to live remains our greatest tool for survival. Little Roy taught me that lesson.

Today, he's completely normal except at barely three years old, he'll hike two miles with his parents. He and I have found Nemo 22 times. He cannot hit a golf ball consistently, but his swing looks Homeric. He smiles a lot and loves having his picture taken. He's another one of those gifts from God who packs tartar sauce in his backpack when you send them out after Moby Dick.

Before exploring the other end of life, let's look at a common challenge many families face. Divorce differs from other hurdles families encounter because, by its very nature, it changes the definition of a family. For many, it's the real toughie.

Children both young and old face divorce every day. Roughly half of all marriages end in divorce. Separating the herring from the backbone often sets kids back in ways that parents didn't anticipate or understand. As a child of divorced parents, forty two years of living have provided me with a perspective that helps separate the trauma of the actual divorce from the considerations families often bring to the subject. Four insights emerged:

1. Teenagers simultaneously facing the onset of puberty and divorce may confuse divorce as a refutation of their very being.
2. Divorce does not mean the end of love between parents.
3. Divorce differs from separation.
4. Divorce does not, and should not, mean that children lose a parent.

Dating the only daughter of a large, brawling, smartass Italian family taught me a lot. Maria's five brothers communicated very clearly in their own charming way that I had better not mess with their sister. She carried a very special place in their hearts—and rightly so. Maria sounded, looked, and felt like a sweet prayer, all of which made the relationship between her grandparents more puzzling to me.

Grandma Giordano lived in a small cottage next to Maria's parents, outside of town. Grandpa Giordano lived in town, above a storefront the family owned. It was near the Italian market and the family barbershop. They would appear together only at family functions, holidays, Sunday Mass, and the school activities of their grandchildren. And yet they remained married.

Maria and her brothers understood that both Grandpa and Grandma could be a handful. In a family of smartasses, these two stood tall. They possessed serpent tongues full of piss and vinegar, and their commentary didn't miss much. So nobody really seemed surprised that the two lived and loved apart. The twinkle in their eyes reminded us of how all of those children and grandchildren had come to be. Separate but married, they remained whole as individuals and as a family. They had a love that didn't bother with what society expects, a love that they built individually and together. In time, I came to understand it and admire it.

Marriages can pass their expiration date. The question becomes what's fair? What would be best for all concerned? Should parents just "gut it out"? Maybe for awhile? Should they thoughtfully separate and postpone the divorce until the rest of the family can process and absorb the need for change? Can divorce be done well?

Each marriage may be different. Yet, each can continue or end in a way that's fair to both people and to the family. In a way that's best for all concerned. At what point can we say its not fair for two people to repair marriage? Death marks the end of life, not the end of the relationship.

In *Tuesdays with Morrie*, Mitch Albom captures a concept that conjures up memories of the crowds lined up outside the funeral home where my own Grandfather lay in repose. Flying up to Michigan as my Grandfather's physical life came to an end, we drove his burgundy Lincoln to the Labadie Funeral Home. This car would drive itself through my father's sleeping dreams for the rest of his life, Grandpa at the wheel.

Automobiles carried special significance to my Dad. As a teenager, he'd seen cars both end a life and provide a sanctuary to begin life. Driving his own father's car to the funeral home underscored for him how Grandpa leaving us physically did not mean for a second that he would really be gone.

Nope.

He lived—lived through the stories told around the dinner table repeatedly referencing his sunny optimism and genuine sense of gratitude and humility. Not being distracted by his corny jokes and stiff drinks actually helped us refine him into what we most valued. His spirit, humanity, and sense of purpose in helping himself, his family, and his tribe stood out more clearly after he died. Death marked the end of his physical presence, but not the end of our relationship with him. Families find their own way to treat one another, and the memory of one another, fairly and with love.

Fair to the Tribe

Much has been made of the book *It Takes a Village to Raise a Child*. When I first heard the title, my eyes rolled firmly back into my head, and not just because of its tone of political correctness. It seemed simplistic, but I'll give the author this much: it helps. The book centers on the supportive nature of community and how children and their families benefit from the cooperative nature of a web of friends, teachers, and neighbors. Being fair to others usually leads to the community being fair in return.

I see it differently. Once you've cleared away your own irrational baggage and established within your family an authentic and honest presence, emotional and spiritual space starts to free up for giving unto others as you would want them to give unto you. Being fair to the tribe seems centered on this most golden of rules. But it starts on the inside. It starts with each of us from within.

Coach John Wooden told me, "If you want a friend, be a friend." Being fair to friends and the larger community starts with a gift measured not in dollars, but in authenticity and intent. Purity breeds more purity. When we're clear in our intent and making it about others, we're repaid manifold.

Think about immigrants finding a neighborhood of fellow Swedes, Irish, Italians, Somalis, Cubans, Mexicans, or Chinese. The acts of starting a business, making a sale, generating a profit, and hiring employees seem like the most basic building blocks of tribal fairness. Just moving represents an act of faith in the Golden Rule. Starting an olive oil business, a laundry, a pub, or an accounting practice in the native language of your friends and neighbors represents an act of faith about how others will treat you. Fairness means actions, not words. It's what we actually do for others, not what we say. That's how I think about being fair to the tribe.

Fair to the Living

Just before Christmas of 1996, we piled the kids into our old Chevy Suburban and drove out to the small town of Dexter, just west of Ann Arbor. On the edge of town, down near the river, sits an innocuous little cabin. Pulling up, I sensed a little bit of danger. Not sure why, I murmured to my wife, "It's cold. Please stay with the kids in the car." I walked up to the side door and knocked. A friendly, bearded face topped by a baseball hat emblazoned with the Stars and Bars bellowed, "You here to pick up the pup? Come on in!"

Sure enough, along with the Springer bitch, Murphy and her five puppies were enough ammo and firepower to launch a quick invasion of Ann Arbor, the University, and most of the neighboring townships.

What a juxtaposition!

Right next to these cute as hell and very alive Springer puppies were tables full of the genuine instruments of death.

Without going into the intricacies of the Second Amendment, let's just say this cabin could fairly be described as a small militia of its own. Briskly making out the check for $125, I thanked the NRA breeder and delivered our new puppy to the back seat of the Suburban and three kids squealing with joy. By the time we arrived home, they had named him Monty, and a loving nine year relationship had begun. How do we explain this kind of bond? How do we explain kids nudging each other aside and picking up Monty to plant him in their beds for a good night's sleep? Feeding and walking him, they seemed to automatically know what he needed. These kids were learning to make it about another living creature and not themselves. Profound, yet profoundly simple at the same time.

Every once in a while, young Lindsey and her mom would remind me and the boys that they felt a little outnumbered. Monty added to the bad math. So, about six years into life with Monty, we arranged for his "niece" to be driven from Michigan to our new home in California. Sitting in the front seat with Jennifer, the college age daughter of family friends, this little lady pup seemed intent on heading west to her new home.

Somewhere along the way, not yet having seen her, Lindsey named her Daisy. She was just what we all (including Daisy) needed. It's hard to believe dogs could have such distinct personalities. Despite being uncle and niece, these two springers could not have been more different. Attentive, sweet, and maybe a bit clingy, she provided our daughter with exactly that feeling of connectedness that was missing for her with Monty.

The boys had Monty.

Lindsey had Daisy.

Family pets serve an important purpose. Thanks to shorter canine and feline life expectancies, they provide a compressed but powerful analog for the full circle of life. Families can learn about fairness when deciding how to potty train a puppy. How long do we let a dog cry while confined to the training cage during the night? What's the best procedure to train a kitten not to chew on furniture and shoes? When does discipline help to train and teach? When is discipline just cruel? How much suffering will we allow for a family pet at the end of her life? How much of a family budget do we devote to treating a failing, elderly Springer Spaniel like Monty or Daisy? Those not earning the coin know no limit. How do we teach or explain when enough is enough?

Monty developed cancer at eight years old. He could not use his hindquarters at the end. Daisy began to wobble and stagger as she developed diabetes at eleven. My wife stayed with Monty until his eyes closed in death. I stayed with Daisy as her heart stopped beating. Lots of Kleenex and Facebook pages full of photos and "Likes" followed. Such emotion surfaces in being fair to the living.

Families see the suffering and learn what's fair. What's fair to Monty. What's fair to Daisy—which doesn't mean we treated them the same. We just treated them both fairly.

Fair to the Environment

Ken Boulding displayed a real talent for asking the provocative, jarring questions. As he explored property rights and their role in providing incentives, he could sense the arid nature of the topic.

"If we're serious about cleaning the water in the Mississippi River, shouldn't we consider selling it to General Electric?"

If his students struggled with the idea of letting children pick their parents, they became totally unglued at the idea of GE making money selling water to the citizens and customers of the Mississippi Delta. Such was the genius of Ken Boulding. He knew how to jar your intellectual senses.

His logical construct flowed nicely:
- We take care of what we own.
- No one owns the environment.
- If someone did, they would take care of it.

- They could sell its use to the rest of us and generate revenue.
- We could use that revenue to invest, manage, and care for it.
- All of us would benefit from their self-interest.

Conundrum would be a kind word for the dilemma we face in taking care of the environment. Simply put, there seems no practical way to endow air and water with property rights. Yet it's worth noting that wealth and cleaner environments tend to go hand in hand. Maybe old Ken Boulding had a point. The greater our stake in the world, the more likely we will keep it clean.

Fair for Seven Generations

Kaianerekowa is possibly the oldest basis for democracy in North America. *The Great Law of Peace* grew from a terrible war between Native American tribes centuries before the Pilgrims. Spawning a new mindset, its creators began to teach their people that for a decision to be wise, it must be fair to seven generations. Being fair to those that come after us? Fair for eternity? Wow! Now we're going bigtime. Let's see if we can

- The Oneida and Cayuga served as its congress.
- Clan mothers served as a kind of judiciary.
- It honored individuals, both living and those not yet born.

The idea of a Great Spirit can seem a little touchy-feely to modern, hardened Americans. In a world of Internet-fueled rage and name calling, fermenting our decisions for seven generations seems almost quaint and antiquated.

Maybe it is, but that doesn't diminish its value to our ability to make the fairest possible decisions.

Consider it this way: even if we agree that fossil fuels will cause irreparable damage, we may need to accept that burning some coal for electricity on our way to solar or wind power may have been justified. Inexpensive and affordable energy allowed large numbers to stay warm, stay cool, and commute to faroff jobs. Cheap energy helps people climb out of poverty. History teaches us the primacy of tradeoffs. Easy decisions rarely show up. In the end, maybe looking at the long term with patience, an open mind, and a sense of balance will best serve the goal of being fair to those seven generations in the future.

This story began with the cliché description of fair as I heard it from an old boss and mentor I remember fondly. Our kids can quote it and roll their eyes all in one motion. It does warrant settling on a working definition, however. Should we put fairness to ourselves first and foremost? What about fairness to family? To coworkers or all living beings? The environment and future generations? Maybe the answer should be a simple yes—fairness to ourselves first. If we cannot be fair to ourselves, we cannot function well enough to be fair across these other domains. It starts from within. Then we can look out to others.

Wouldn't a reasonable definition of fair be the good faith effort to find balance? How about trying to consider each affected group and find a solution that works reasonably well for everyone?

We could consider the founding of the American Republic and its democratic organs of governance, which balance one against another. Similarly, the United Nations was founded with an emphasis on inclusion and institutional balance. Lasting progress means accepting the best combination in a mélange or mix of serious tradeoffs. A senior mentor once offered that "the quest for perfection can be the enemy of progress." Or, my personal favorite, "better to be approximately right than precisely wrong."

I find peace of mind in accepting just such a fair and realistic approach to life.

37

Profiles in Cookies

In 2003, I lost two fathers. In April, my own father succumbed to a rare form of bronchitis. His passing was a blessing in a way, as he had fought the disease for years and just couldn't hold out any longer. My father-in-law's death that August felt very different. The closing of his mind predated by many years the closing of his life. Alzheimer disease can take the light out of a life the way a long sunset closes the day. It proceeds so slowly, you almost miss that final moment. My eyes still moisten with the memories.

After all of us spoke our piece at the memorial service for Matthew Donald Rutherford Riddell, we lounged around the living room with ties loosened and shoes strewn around the hall. Group sadness gets old very fast, so I pulled some old yearbooks from the living room shelves. Sure enough, I found his Harvard annual from 1965, twenty five years after his graduation from the Yard.

Most of the book consists of men outlining their roles as captains of industry, law, and medicine: as a group, they seemed to truly believe that they shit marble. Not my father-in-law. That simply didn't suit his genuine humility and sense of decorum. Nope, he spent his paragraph describing very different kinds of accomplishments.

Don (I know, too many Dons for one book) Riddell described his children's love of Boy Scouts and Brownies. Rather than drone endlessly about his leadership of—say—an esteemed civil and environmental engineering firm, he described the badges his children had earned scouting in Glenview, Illinois. He mentioned the prodigious cookie sales of young Ann Rutherford Riddell, and his pride came from a very sunny and authentic place. He also managed to put in a plug for the fundraising efforts of Dorothy, his librarian wife, on behalf of the new Glenview Public Library. What a grand and gracious guy—so easy to like, so easy to love and trust.

The inside cover page of that album only added to the sense of Don's genuine humility. As it was 1965, it was only appropriate that the Class of 1940 would include a dedication to their slain classmate, President John F. Kennedy. As I looked at his picture as a graduate in 1940, time seemed to stand still.

How could such a young man meet such a fate? Hundreds of books attempt to explain the hate and animus behind the assassination plot. For his classmates, however, Kennedy would always be "Jack," a guy everyone seemed to like.

During the summer of 1960, Jack Kennedy arrived at their twentieth Reunion looking for votes and donors. Finding plenty of both put candidate Kennedy in a jovial mood. When he ran into his old classmate, Don Riddell, he could only remark, "Thanks, Don, for getting me through calculus!" And what really made the family smile: "Don, we may be the only two guys in Winthrop House who still have a full head of hair." It's safe to say that the Republican leaning Riddells voted Republican in 1960; still, it was tough to resist the persuasive skills of John F. Kennedy.

Recounting the life of Don Riddell will strike readers as a school smart version of Forrest Gump. Don came into the world in Toronto, in 1918. Born to Scottish parents from Edinburgh, he took his status as an only child very seriously. His mother had learned the ways of proper society as a nanny to the J. P & Coats family in highbrow Edinburgh. His father, Matthew, earned his doctorate in engineering and pioneered some of the early wing designs for the De Havilland Aircraft Company. His father's work at the University of Toronto led the University of Illinois to recruit him to found the aeronautics program within their engineering college. This move landed young Don Riddell at the University School in Urbana, Illinois. What a lucky break!

University High boasts a long list of esteemed graduates including Pulitzer award recipients and Nobel Prize winners like George F. Will and James Tobin. Yet it was young Don Riddell who earned valedictorian honors. Luck can take many forms. For young Don, it came from a thoughtful teacher who encouraged him and his good friend, Jim Tobin, to sit for an examination that ultimately led to their Harvard scholarships—the only way the Riddells could afford to send Don to Cambridge. Don and Jim took the train to the Chicago

Armory where the exam was administered, and their acceptance and scholarship letters arrived about sixty days later. Don always appreciated that teacher who had taken the time to send him and his buddy to that exam. Plus, they took in the Cubs game before they boarded the train back to Urbana—what a life-changing day. It made all the difference.

Attending Harvard also included training in the naval officer's program on campus. Not long after his graduation, Don found himself as a junior turret officer on a large battleship. The peculiar part of the story was the repainting and flagging of the USS Alabama as the HMS Black Knight. Why? Well, old FDR could be a slippery customer.

To get around the Neutrality Act, ships like the Alabama draped themselves in British paint and flags. Don served with other officers and sailors from Commonwealth countries like Australia, New Zealand, and Canada. Serving the Commonwealth took on a whole new meaning as they helped protect the convoys of American and British ships bringing badly needed supplies to Britain and Russia, all part of FDR's determined effort to keep these allies in the war. The North Atlantic can be cold as hell. The run to Murmansk in the Soviet Union was its own kind of Cold War.

Serving out of Scapa Flow, Scotland, Lieutenant Junior Grade Don Riddell found himself back in the family homeland. He remarked about his nervousness when he shook hands with Lord Mountbatten during Sunday Church Parade, Thanksgiving of 1940. Prying these precious moments out of Don became a labor of love—a love that lives to this day.

The tragedy at Pearl Harbor meant rerouting the Black Knight to Hawaii for new paint, new flags, new American uniforms, and higher pay as officers of the great battle wagon Alabama. Joining the Fleet after the Battle of Midway, Don served dutifully as a Turret Officer on the 'Bama until his transfer late in 1944 to the USS Chicago. Don's wife, Dorothy, told me privately that his only extended leave came with the death of his mother—a trip to Urbana to stand with his father at her grave. "Never complain; never explain" describes him very well.

Don freely offered that the heavy cruiser USS Chicago mostly provided protection to the big carriers during the first half of 1945. Shore bombardment ended when she escorted the Missouri to Tokyo Bay for the surrender and the occupation of Honshu. The Chicago provided a base for artifact work after the Japanese armistice and before the signing of the surrender. Don used to show his grandkids the sword and revolver that he kept as souvenirs from his time on the artifact crew. He described extensively the rapid and complete conversion of the defeated Japanese to deferential citizens. It always seemed to baffle Don that after years of fighting, the warring sides established peaceful relations so quickly. The craziest part was learning, walking through a receiving line after the surrender signing, that Lord Mountbatten remembered Matthew Donald Rutherford Riddell from five years earlier. Remarkable.

We only saw one really emotional window open with Don. When the USS Chicago steamed into the harbor at San Pedro, California, he knew he'd survived—and he let out tears of genuine satisfaction, salted by a deep sense of relief.

Before Don returned to the City of Chicago, where his journey to college began, he finished his graduate work in environmental engineering at Harvard. Staying near to his only family—his father, Matthew—guided him back to the Midwest. Greeley & Hanson is a high end consulting firm focused primarily on civil and sanitation engineering work. Luck would put Don Riddell in the archive room, where young Dorothy Williams worked as the firm's librarian. Funny how he kept needing assistance with various drawings, plans, and files. Mischievously, Don laid tack paper down on Dorothy's library shelves, just so she would come down to his office and lay into him…

A year later, they married.

Nine months after that blessed event—to the day...James Donald Riddell arrived in the world. Twenty two months after Jim, David Williams Riddell arrived. Ann Rutherford became the "caboose," five years after David.

Many countries can lay claim to a "greatest generation." America pivoted from helping Britain and the Soviet Union survive, and by the end of the war had accepted the mantle of world leader. For this greatest generation, the goal was much simpler.

Don and Dorothy Riddell survived the Great Depression. They remained clear, clean, and humble. They would be good in their hearts. They would do their best for their children, their neighbors, and their fellow citizens. Striving to be fair on all these levels provided them a homegrown compass—profiles in cookies, Little League, and libraries.

38

Tower to America

Standing 205 feet above the highlands of Florida and representing its highest point, the Bok Tower signals more than just an architectural achievement. It stands as a loving monument to our American ideals. Conceived by Edward Bok and designed by Frederick Law Olmsted Jr. and Milton Medary, our "Taj Mahal" seems to inspire a set of values and principles much more noble and enduring than its pink marble, coquina, and carillon bells. Edward Bok must be smiling down on his winter home community and nearby Lake Wales as they reinvent themselves. A community shedding its failed public policies of the 1960s, Lake Wales is changing right before our eyes. Florida's Shangri La can provide a lofty vantage point for interested Americans who wonder if there can be life after the partisan philosophical battles of the last fifty three years. The lessons are worth considering.

Edward Bok wrote an autobiography, *The Americanization of Edward Bok,* that candidly described how America fell short for him and why he owed it so much. Wonderfully simple and straightforward, Bok gives our American experiment a very fair shake.

"Where America Fell Short With Me"

Young Bok brought to America a thorough familiarity with the importance of thrift, an aversion to debt, and an affinity for work done completely and thoroughly. Born in the Netherlands in 1863 and arriving in New York just before

his seventh birthday, Bok carried with him these Old World values. Dutch businesses thrived for centuries on the back of guild tradesmen and skilled artisans like him. Bok explains,

> As a Dutch boy, one of the cardinal truths taught me was that whatever was worth doing was worth doing well; that next to honesty came thoroughness as a factor in success. It was not enough that anything should be done; it was not to be done at all if it was not done well. The two infernal Americanisms "That's good enough" and "That will do" were taught to me, together with the maxim of quantity rather than quality. (Page 535)

This lack of thoroughness permeates much of our American thinking. Theodore Roosevelt nailed it as our "real curse." Bok makes the connection of this American character flaw to how we educate our youth. Our unwillingness to teach foreign-born children the English language completely and thoroughly plagued Bok as a young boy. The homonyms and synonyms of standard English can haunt those trying to learn our language, and Bok, depending on his father for remedial time and attention, understood just how dysfunctional public education in America can be. He experienced it firsthand.

What an irony that just eighty years after his tower to America was erected, its namesake, the Bok Academy, would form as the Lake Wales school district converted to charter status. The system consists of a network of quality elementary schools, Bok Academy Middle School, Lake Wales High School, and an International Baccalaureate World School.

Rising in prominence as the teachers and students perfect what it means to educate young people, Lake Wales has in nine short years transformed itself from a failing school district to one of Florida's finest. The district scores high on statewide exams and is recognized for a very strong STEM curriculum that netted it an award as an "Apple Exemplary School." One more piece of evidence that culture, values, and principles can overcome even the most intransigent of political forces and vested interests. Part of Florida's distinction rests within their actual charter district and school conversion legislation. Charter districts and schools must be administered by not for profit organizations. For profit educational companies need not apply.

"What I Owe to America"

Bok conveys—in an authentic voice of gratitude—that he knows no country offers its immigrants opportunities like America. In his own words:

[An American] can go where he will; no traditions hamper him; no limitations are set except this within himself. The larger the vision he demonstrates, the more eager the people are to give support this undertaking if they are convinced that he has their best welfare as his goal. There is no public confidence equal to that of the American public, once it is obtained. (Page 549)

Let's deconstruct Bok just a bit. He asserts that "no limitations are set except within himself." Right off the bat, he focuses the reader within themselves as the font of inspiration and drive. In the words of the bible, "the Kingdom of God is within us." Bok underscores this central tenet of the American experiment. Most of the answers lie within us. When we free ourselves of the doubts and apprehensions that haunt our psyches, we free up space for inspiration, imagination, and making a mark in the world.

He extends this line of reasoning by suggesting that we distinguish ourselves through "the vision we demonstrate." It's not just what we can imagine and conceive, it's what we do, what we make and create, what we demonstrate that matters. Entrepreneurs makes their mark through actions and work, not just words. Further, "the more eager the people are to give support this undertaking *if they are convinced that he has their best welfare as his goal.*" Bok could see clearly, more than a hundred years ago, that it's the entrepreneur's ability to make his or her work about the "welfare of others" that leads to great success. It parallels the thinking of twenty-first century business builders like Steve Jobs, John Mackey of Whole Foods, and Herb Kelleher of Southwest Airlines. A hundred years ago, Bok could see these concepts. Such were the ideals and principles that built Edward Bok's love tower to America.

"Bok as a Servant Leader"

Bok understood the enduring and giving nature of leadership. He built the tower as an expression of love of country. However, it also stands as a monument to his inspired brand of generous servant leadership—lessons this author learned in a very different context.

Servant leadership for me came in observing our eldest so as he applied to college. Our son Mark dreamed for many years of attending one of the national service academies. After enduring the long application process and being accepted academically, one last step remained. He would be required to secure a nomination from a senator or congressman. Our congressman could only nominate two that year, so he set up a selection board consisting of retired military officers in the area, and a dozen students showed up on a Saturday morning in January to be interviewed.

Arriving home, Mark slumped into the living room couch. I tried (as casually as a pushy Papa can) to ask him how it had gone. High school seniors can be pretty reticent with nosy parents, but Mark finally offered, "Dad, it was just like you said. They asked me about leadership—'What's your definition of leadership?'—and so I told them about what we read in that book by Mr. Hunter, *The Servant.*"

My mind scrambled to remember what James Hunter had written. Mark piped up. "Recognize the legitimate needs of the people for whom you're responsible, and serve those needs with great passion and enthusiasm." Whew! I was so proud—even if I could have remembered that concept, I doubt I could have recited it under the pressure of that august interviewing board. Mark nailed it and was commissioned four and a half years later under the watchful eyes of our newly inaugurated president, Barack Obama.

Bok understood that the readers of the *Ladies Home Journal* needed more than fashion, cosmetics, and cooking ideas. They wanted to be informed about birth control, women's health issues, and how to be an effective parent and spouse. He aimed high. Bok transformed the magazine into a "must have" publication for women at the beginning of the 20th century. It became almost equivalent to Oprah today. He served their legitimate needs, and as publisher did it with painstaking research, enthusiasm, and generosity of spirit.

He brought the same spirit to his winter home in Lake Wales. He found *the highest ground*. He hired the best architects in Frederick Olmsted and Milton Medary. Using only the finest native marble and coquina, he built it to last. He integrated the civic notion of carillon bells into the tower, giving it the nickname, "The Singing Tower." He endowed it financially in perpetuity, and then gave it to the State of Florida. To this day, the tower imbues all who can see it and hear the carillon's melodies with that spiritual sense of being connected to the larger world and its legitimate needs. Bok demonstrated in the grandest possible way what servant leadership really looks like.

Changing the Cultural Landscape

Towering 205 feet above its 308 elevation and base of gardens and ponds, the tower now represents a great deal to its neighboring communities and to Florida as a whole. Leaders can now draw inspiration from it and communicate clearly and powerfully how things should be done, how they should look, and what the future should look like. Lake Wales did not just conceive and build a single charter school. It converted a whole school district to charter status. Change of this magnitude confounds conventional description. This represents knocking over the apple cart, throwing away the old cart, and selling a new kind of apple. Once you create a whole district that skyrockets from one of the lowest performing in Florida to one of the top two or three performing in the area, you've entered a whole new dynamic.

This newly reconstituted school district now has begun to transform the larger community. All of the educators in the charter system immersed themselves "all in" toward the pursuit of teaching all students. Those who chose not to get on board were asked to leave. What remained were educators with the mindset that every child can learn, and every child matters. That mindset is now evident in the young men and women exiting the pride filled halls of Lake Wales High School. Some choose to stay right in their backyard and attend the new STEM state university that recently opened. Florida Polytechnic University may someday be as large and excellent as the University of Florida or Georgia Tech.

New employers like State Farm and Geico are moving into the area. Transplants and snowbirds are beginning to choose the highlands of Florida instead of the coastal communities. Triggering that kind of enduring and thorough change would make the immigrant boy proud of how transformative an American community can become. It starts with leadership and is extended by a culture that leaders can spread and impart to the next generation. This version of the American Dream becomes more ennobling every day.

Settling into a winter home for the last act of my own life, I could never have anticipated the lessons I would learn in my late fifties under the shade of the Bok Tower—a remote spot close to Eden and closer to that clearing within us. I was lucky to be born on third base—in America, halfway through the twentieth century; I remind myself regularly: I didn't hit a triple.

39

27 Hands

Soon after settling into my new home in Mountain Lake, the harsh reality of nearby Lake Wales and surrounding Polk County came as a bit of a shock. The majestic Bok Tower looks over the Park which is local slang for Mountain Lake. If Ann Arbor and Boulder can be fairly described as a few square miles of utopia surrounded by reality, Mountain Lake earns that moniker in a far more literal way. Frederick Olmsted designed a beauty, but it's very much an island of prosperity within a larger area marked by widespread working class poverty. My first direct exposure came at a dinner held in the Park at the Colony House, which functions as the community hall. The dinner honored and featured artwork, music and poetry created by the students of the Lake Wales Charter School District. It was an eye opener.

Seated next to an esteemed teacher from the high school, I heard directly and in detail the curriculum of the International Baccalaureate program. The number of students involved and the percentages of students earning course proficiencies, and the percentage earning the full IB degree. Amazing when you consider that over 65% of students qualify for the federal free lunch subsidy and nearly 40% free lunch and breakfast. The artwork caught my eye. The poetry struck a chord. The Bach concerto moistened my eyes. For the son of a school teacher, these accomplished students won me over with the purity of their effort.

The principal of the middle school soon became a good friend. Damien Moses earned All-American honors as a defensive tackle at South Carolina State. With two degrees in hand, he returned to central Florida to serve the young students of Polk County and Lake Wales. Kids just call him "Moses". Kids always seem to know.

His right hand within the Bok Academy, Dr. Lubertha DiPrimo invited me to her classroom one day to describe the training and teaching I had done at J.P. Morgan and other Wall Street investment houses. By late February, we began a ten week Oration and Public Speaking workshop for eighth graders soon heading to high school, and completely consumed with adolescent spring fever.

Beginning with the actual video recordings of Dr. Martin Luther King, Steve Jobs and Margaret Thatcher we began to see that even great orators exhibited certain strengths and weaknesses. We learned from Aristotle and his rubric of ethos ~ pathos ~ logos in crafting sophisticated persuasion, and refining it to a high standard of effectiveness. Within three weeks, Dr. DiPrimo and I scheduled the presentation days and began coaching the youngsters as they selected their topics and began laying out their pitches and communication.

Presentation week included many topics you'd expect to hear from 13 year olds about to enter high school. Students pitched us on why "Cheer" should be a varsity sport. Computer games should be a class offered in the curriculum. The school lunches should include more protein and fewer carbohydrates. Logos shined through with their linear and sequential ordering of their evidence and data. We could feel the ethos of their actual experience inside the issues they described. However, it was a young woman and a young man whose emotional courage allowed us to see their pathos, and it made us as adults gulp...hard.

The young man had lost his mother to breast cancer a year earlier when he was 12 years old. The young woman saw her grandfather experience elder abuse in the home until one day when he didn't wake up after suffering a beating. Their courage and strength of character shone through their concise selection of words. They even managed some purposeful hand gestures and moist eye contact. The kids won big that week. Although the young man cried privately with me after class, he came to realize that he was stronger for telling his story.

More than adults I had trained and coached, many of these young people wanted to come clean emotionally, and reveal themselves. Of all places, they unmasked themselves in front of their peers. They had begun to "clear" these difficult memories. I hadn't fully realized that an eighth grader is part adult and part child. We got lucky. Aristotle and his triad of ethos ~ logos ~ pathos fit where these kids were developmentally. A child wants to tell us what happened. An adult can craft the story from the viewpoint of the audience. 13 year olds can, in many ways, be at the ideal age for this kind of instruction and self counsel.

As a byproduct of this coursework, we could hear and see that a percentage of students in each classroom could not read effectively at an eighth grade level. In each of six sections there were 4-5 kids who struggled to read their own words and the texts we began to read from the autobiography of Edward Bok. Some of the struggling readers had transferred into Bok Academy. Some came to the school through the "school choice" program Tallahassee created. After a few more weeks, I hazarded the question. "Should we think about offering a Reading Camp this summer? Would kids sign up and show up? Could we pull it off?"

Dr. DiPrimo may be short in stature, but she is long in enthusiasm and planning out the details. School classrooms were reserved. Breakfasts and lunches were ordered. Transportation schedules arrived in the mail from the school bus offices. Funds were raised and books were considered. "Old Man of the Sea", "Hidden Figures" (eventually chosen in 2017) and the Jackie Robinson autobiography "My Own Story" became serious contenders. The criteria became the quality of the writing, the vocabulary, and the appropriateness of the content for eighth graders.

We chose the Jackie Robinson autobiography, in part, because of the beautiful, genuine and honest relationship between Robinson and the iconic President of the Brooklyn Dodgers Branch Rickey. This relationship changed baseball and these students could see, in Jackie's own words, that they did it the right way.

On the first day, with only five minutes of fanfare and ground rules, we headed to our classrooms and began to read. Out loud, word by word, one at a time, we spent two and a half weeks reading every line and breaking down the prefixes and suffixes of all the unfamiliar vocabulary. If a student let their mind wander off, we called on them next. Everybody read and most everybody paid attention. On the second to last day, we brought in popcorn and root beer, closed the shades, turned off the lights and watched the movie "42". Chadwick Boseman and Harrison Ford captured so movingly the pathos and affection of Robinson and Branch Rickey. Robinson living the Christian ethic of "turning the other cheek". Rickey telling the racist owner of the Philadelphia Phillies that "someday you will meet your Maker and when He asks you why you didn't take the field against Robinson and you tell him that it's because he was a Negro...THAT MAY NOT BE A SUFFICIENT REPLY!!!"

These two American heroes exemplified everything young people can hold as good and virtuous. The kids came to love both of them as historical figures. White kids revering a black man. Black kids revering a white man. Racial reconciliation found another home. The final day brought one final offering.

That last morning, we boarded a Lake Wales school bus and drove the hour and a half to Daytona Beach, site of the Jackie Robinson ballpark and museum. Home to the AA minor league Daytona Reds, this ballpark housed the Brooklyn Dodgers for spring training that February of 1947 when Robinson signed his first major league contract. The minor league radio announcers served that day as docents. They began leading us through the various stanchions which displayed the life and history of Jackie Robinson.

When we stopped in front of the stanchion showing Jackie in his UCLA track uniform winning the long jump, the docent asked if the kids knew about Robinson's education? 27 Hands went up, "he attended high school in Pasadena, California". "He played in the same high school football backfield with the Heisman Trophy winner Glenn Davis". "He graduated from UCLA and commissioned as an Army officer in WW II". The docent gulped and looked at his partner as they raised their eyebrows high and tight.

Next, we stopped at a stanchion depicting Robinson signing his major league contract under the proud gaze of Branch Rickey. The docent then tentatively asked, "does anyone know who Branch Rickey was?". 27 more hands rose. "He was a player and coach at Ohio Wesleyan and the University of Michigan. He saw racial discrimination first hand as it laid low his black teammates". "After law school, he joined the St. Louis Browns. He knew, even then, he needed to do more". "Later, as president of the Brooklyn Dodgers he saw the business opportunity."

At this point, the docents asked the questions, while they let the kids do the talking. On the bus trip back, my heart was warmed by the proud chatter of the kids. All of us formed loose groups, and played gin rummy returning to Lake Wales. I couldn't help but think that Jackie and Branch would be pleased with our summer of planning, preparation and teaching. A remote school district in central Florida kept their good work alive for 27 more hands.

40
Ann Arbor Train

S pending the summers on the old west side of Ann Arbor offers many midlife advantages. You don't need to buy an alarm clock. The Ann Arbor Railroad sending its trains through downtown around 6:00 am functions as a perfect substitute. Leaving a window open absolutely insures you'll be snatched out of your personal dreamland and deep REM sleep. You can walk for fresh morning locally sourced (or at least ground) coffee and muffins. Lunching on a Blimpy burger keeps your GI system working all afternoon. Twilight walks for Washtenaw Dairy ice cream becomes a difficult habit to break. West End Grill may be a tad pricey for regular dining, however, its natural ingredients make it memorable and flavorful every time. Evening taverns offer only a short stagger home and Happy Hours typically run from 4:00 – 6:00 pm. The aging rock 'n roll band Fubar at Live and graying dancers work it good the first Friday night of every month. Even midnight munchies can be adequately handled by the Fleetwood Diner. This Woebegone neighborhood seems tough to beat. Everybody and everything that is midlife seems solidly above average.

Welcome to one half of America. The half that operates in a series of perfectly organic but very well planned urban utopias. This half of America erects yard signs like mini-billboards to remind you of their purity and goodness. How else would you know to shut down the Enbridge Pipeline 5 that runs under the Mackinac Bridge shipping crude oil from Canada and Michigan's Upper Peninsula to the lower 48? Higher pay for teachers, amnesty for Dreamers, "Stop the Hate"—you can fill out a political ballot with just one trip through such a neighborhood. It seems unlikely that yard signs will actually move the heart and soul of America. Yet, here it's clearly a growth industry. Maybe, we're just mumbling to ourselves.

In America's other half, we see fewer yard signs and more economic stress. Yard signs qualify as a luxury for many of these home dwellers. Their Dreamers face a world of student debt, fewer school choices and diminished expectations. These working class families know diseases like Mesothelioma, Legionnaires, and onset diabetes. Opioids make for addictive recreation. In one such county in Ohio, the working class electorate of Trumbull went from voting overwhelmingly for Barack Obama to voting overwhelmingly for Donald Trump. These are desperate voters. $20 trillion of recently added government debt serves as an useful reminder of their desperation. The only thing more annoying than listening to Donald Trump is the realization that about 27% of what he says is true and accurate.

The dichotomy of America today can seem unbridgeable. The snarling personalities on cable television earn market share by more effectively and vociferously demonizing the other side. Condescension and contempt long ago replaced comity and compromise. The ironies become too numerous to list. That morning train running through the near west side of Ann Arbor pulls long lines of petroleum tanker cars. Ask the former citizens of Lac Megantic, Quebec if they would prefer a pipeline submerged 100' under water to trains pulling tankers through a densely populated urban area. Sorry, not enough of Lac Megantic exists anymore to ask.

Imagine a dozen petroleum tankers derailing one block from the taverns and restaurants along Ann Arbor's downtown

Liberty Street, and a block from the Victorian era wood frame homes of the historic Old West Side. Amidst the flames and explosions, the yard signs wouldn't stand a chance. Victorian homes make ideal kindling. The pedestrians that fill these streets and alleyways would literally be running for their lives.

The automobile workers union (UAW) gave Trumbull County, Ohio and other working class areas a vibrant middle class in the 1950's. Government employee unions in the 1990's and 2000's bankrupted cities like Flint, Michigan leaving them unable to fund and finance a functioning water system. Just when we think the answers all come from the Right or the Left, we see the fallacies permeating much of our political ideologies. It may not be that the answers lie in the middle.

Practical answers do not lie with ideology. Maybe the most enduring legislative responses emerge more from a process and not a political platform. Maybe the Founding Fathers knew that debate, discourse, and seeing the problem from the opposition's point of view formed the predicate for genuine progress in public policy. Maybe they knew that making it more difficult to pass a law would necessitate a process that created more lasting laws.

Seeing the world from the opposition's point of view can be difficult. It may be a sign of maturity and rationality; yet, our own pent up frustrations and snubs can be hard to set aside. Social media fuels this beast. That may be why we seek cozy neighborhoods where people think the way we do and plant similar yard signs. It's just easier that way. We're left just mumbling to one another.

When I walk to the Argus Farm Stop for coffee, my golf attire makes me a bit of an anomaly. A golfer who walks a golf course still looks sufficiently bourgeois to be déclassé on the near west side. Yet, fellow customers and staff seem to see me as an individual once they get past my appearance. The same could be said of them. Even though some dress like potato farmers from the Ukraine, in fact, some are actual farmers.

They often don't fit into the neat tidy political identity group we associate with that particular style of clothing. How do we get past the first layer? How do we suspend judgement long enough to learn more and want to learn more about one another?

In the last section of this book, we met Lily Edelman and Slaw Radomski. Neither of these figures fit a mold. Maybe that's the secret sauce. Loving and accepting our own foibles allows us to accept the same in others. Discernment is different than assessment. Discernment requires suspending judgement. Understanding before we comment. Seeing life from the other bloke's point of view helps to rest our own mind. Merely by stepping into another person's shoes calms our own charged mindset and world view. Giving us pause. It opens our heart. Warms the soul. Generosity flows.

Epilogue: Christmas

As our grand Godson, Roy, sat on Santa's lap for a photo at the nearby shopping mall, an odd smile and look lit his face. It's as if he understood that it's smart to believe in Santa. Sometimes, life strikes me that way.

One year, in the annual report for the Investment Company of America, our investors' relations team highlighted the oldest living shareholders in the fund. This husband and wife lived a comfortable but circumspect retirement on Martha's Vineyard. In the accompanying photograph, they wore glowing smiles, looking the part of a content couple at peace in the sunset of their life. The husband had inherited a very modest fund balance while he attended college on the GI Bill after serving in World War II. He finished his graduate studies and taught economics at Columbia for over forty years. His wife taught psychology at Hofstra and retired soon after her husband.

Despite his considerable training in quantitative analytical economics, this sage economist offered advice that seemed stunningly qualitative and simple.

"It pays to be an optimist."

I couldn't say it better myself.

But let me try. The nub of the professor's wisdom rests in his concision, his simplicity, and his sunny faith in the future. Thinking back to Roosevelt, Kennedy, and Reagan, this seems to be the secret sauce. Add in the importance of keeping an open mind and a loving heart. We begin the path toward a heart slow to judge and punctual with forgiveness. We see ourselves and the world around us with fewer dark clouds and long shadows. A crystal clear future awaits those who make themselves ready.

Kirk D. Dodge began writing as daily calisthenics at Greenhills School in Ann Arbor, and continued honing his craft at the University of Colorado with the encouragement of Professor Lawrence Singell.

He works and lives in Mountain Lake, Florida. Summers include the Bok Academy Reading Camp, the Old West Side of Ann Arbor and the sandy meadows of Benzie County. Collecting stories from all the jagged and bumpy edges of life, he writes every morning, allowing him to compose his mind and untangle life's secrets and mysteries.

Don W. Placek is a Senior Golf Course Design Associate with Tom Doak at Renaissance Golf Design Inc. in Traverse City, Michigan. Don attended the University of Colorado/Boulder on an Eisenhower-Evans Caddie Scholarship earning his degree in Environmental Design (BEnvd), not long after the author completed his work at CU in Economics.